# Ascension

Printed in the USA
CPSIA information can be obtained
at www.ICGtesting.com
CBHW031652200324
5621CB00005B/86

# Ascension

*The Sociology of an African American Family's Generational Journey*

Lois Benjamin

The University of North Carolina Press CHAPEL HILL

Set in Merope Basic by Westchester Publishing Services
Manufactured in the United States of America

Library of Congress Cataloging-in-Publication Data

Names: Benjamin, Lois, 1944– author.
Title: Ascension : the sociology of an African American family's generational
    journey / Lois Benjamin.
Other titles: Sociology of an African American family's generational journey
Description: Chapel Hill : The University of North Carolina Press, [2024] |
    Includes bibliographical references and index.
Identifiers: LCCN 2023047029 | ISBN 9781469678665 (cloth ; alk. paper) |
    ISBN 9781469678672 (pbk. ; alk. paper) | ISBN 9781469678689 (ebook) |
    ISBN 9798890887023 (pdf)
Subjects: LCSH: James family. | African American families—North Carolina. |
    African Americans—North Carolina—Social conditions. | BISAC: SOCIAL SCIENCE /
    Ethnic Studies / American / African American & Black Studies | SOCIAL SCIENCE /
    Sociology / General
Classification: LCC E185.86.B3788 2024 | DDC 306.85/089960730756—dc23/eng/20231025
    LC record available at https://lccn.loc.gov/2023047029

Cover illustrations: *Foreground*, oak tree sketch © iStock.com/Bitter;
*background*, watercolor landscape © iStock.com/smodj.

This book will be made open access within three years of publication thanks to Path
to Open, a program developed in partnership between JSTOR, the American Council of
Learned Societies (ACLS), the University of Michigan Press, and the University of North
Carolina Press to bring about equitable access and impact for the entire scholarly community,
including authors, researchers, libraries, and university presses around the world. Learn more
at https://about.jstor.org/path-to-open/.

*In memory*
*of*
*Roscoe James Sr.*
*Pennie Ann James*
*Lubertha Elizabeth James*
*Karen Leola James*

# Contents

## Figures and Table

# Foreword

"It's a rare condition, this day and age, to read any good news, on the newspaper page, the loving tradition of the Grand Design, some people say it's even harder to find."

The introductory lyrics of the *Family Matters* theme song are refrains I grew up with in which I grew up. Its message rings truer to me as I have made my career as a journalist working in newspapers across the East Coast. Although we have more information and technology available to us than ever before in the history of humankind and although we can travel to the moon and connect with people across the globe, if the year 2020 has taught us anything, it is that we still struggle with the basics. That includes loving our neighbors, looking out for one another, and treating others with respect, humility, and grace. A few years ago, when Dr. Lois Benjamin told me about the most recent project she was working on, I listened eagerly as she told me about the family who made her feel more at home than she had ever experienced.

I had good reason. Dr. Benjamin, at heart, is a teacher and a nurturer. Like the plants she kept in her office at Hampton University, she made time to water and grow the minds of her students, pruning with discipline as needed and always offering the sunlight of hope and goodwill to all who were under her tutelage. One of the products of the garden of her career in academia was me. She could look below the surface of any student and see the potential that lay beneath with their personal story. Dr. Benjamin pushed me outside of my comfort zone to help me reach the potential she saw in me. Sometimes that came with a gentle touch, offered with a soothing cup of tea or chlorophyll-infused, distilled water as we sat and listened to classical records that would play as she worked. Sometimes it came with a healthy dose of chastisement. Once when I tried to submit a paper that did not reach her lofty standards, she wrote a note that said "See me" at the top, which indicated I would not receive any grade until my work met with her satisfaction. I have long felt that same tug when I do my current work as a journalist. Is it reaching the potential that Dr. Benjamin and so many of my mentors saw in me?

It is of no small coincidence that Dr. Benjamin felt drawn to the story of the James family. A family overflowing with the infectious love and remarkable resilience that she documents throughout the pages of this book. A family that with little means but abundant spirit wrote their own American story of triumph. The James family generously shared with her their own hard-earned wisdom and the key to their success through some of the most trying of times. Understanding what enabled this family to thrive, not only from a narrative but from an academic and philosophical perspective, may offer more sunlight for our communities as we face trying times once more. As a reporter, much of my work tends to stress the questions around "what?" In the work I see from Dr. Benjamin, the more important concept is the "why?" And the bigger challenge is figuring out "how?"

We know that there is much work to do as we rebuild our society from the ravages of disease and the poison of division and polarization. The inchoate task may at times seem daunting.

Is there a better way forward? Maybe one of the keys lies within our own hearts and homes. In one of the latter *Star Trek* sequels, the state of peace is called the "Undiscovered Country." The a cappella group Sweet Honey in the Rock sings, "When there is peace in the home, there is strength in the nation."

In the James family, Dr. Benjamin discovered a blueprint that might lead us forward as we "seek the loving tradition of the Grand Design."

Austin Brett Bogues
2021 Nieman Fellow in Journalism,
Harvard University and
Assistant Washington Editor, *USA Today*

# Acknowledgments

From start to finish, conducting research and writing *Ascension* over several years required more effort, goodwill, solidarity, and support than could be proffered by myself. I received much encouragement and helpful suggestions from colleagues, friends, and family. First and foremost, I owe a special debt of gratitude to the James family for sharing their collective and individual stories. I am especially indebted to Samuel James who understood the value of his family story and gently nudged me to tell it. From this project's original conception as a newspaper article to its evolution as a book, Samuel always believed that a tome would come to fruition. After reading a draft of my proposed newspaper article, Dr. Zina T. McGee glanced at me and firmly exclaimed, "This is not a newspaper article; it is a book." Although it was not what I desired to hear at the time, I am eternally grateful for my friend's encouragement and support, her helpful comments on several drafts, especially her insights on conceptual modeling and her technical and graphical analysis throughout this process. In reinforcing the idea that a book was in the making, I thank my beloved sister Bernice, who is possessed with the keenest mother wit, for her lifelong love, support, and belief in me. I am also indebted to my longtime friend Sheila Stevens whose vision for this work also extended beyond a newspaper article. She read several drafts of this manuscript and provided critical and helpful feedback, especially with reference to conceptualizing values. In this vein, I thank Lawrence Jones who read several drafts of this work, listened patiently, and offered his emotional, intellectual, and moral support as well as technical assistance.

After much soul searching, I concurred that a newspaper article would not suffice as a platform for the James family's story. Here, I acknowledge my immense debt to Austin Brett Bogues, abled collaborator and former student, who generously read several versions of this manuscript and willingly offered editorial assistance and provided invaluable insights and suggestions, including the addition of chapter 1. His contributions improved this work. I would like to express my deep appreciation to my sister Martha Benjamin for her committed, enthusiastic, and untiring dedication to carefully proofreading various drafts of this manuscript. I am especially grateful for the support and invaluable contribution by Valerie W. James who read a draft of this work and offered helpful comments. She was also instrumental in providing supportive technical and graphical services, especially with photographic and conceptual modeling. She always responded with enthusiasm in a timely manner. I would like to thank Sharon Hardy for her technical service inputting the endnotes. I would also like to acknowledge Chrystal Bucchioni, the adult services librarian at the Newport News Public Library, for her assistance. I am, too, appreciative of the encouragement and the thoughtful suggestions of my friend Claudia Widdiss while working on this book.

Finally, I extend my heartfelt thanks to members of the editorial and production team at the University of North Carolina Press for their supportive acts of collaboration, collective spirit, advice, and suggestion. Specifically, I thank Mark Simpson-Vos, editorial director, and Lucas Church, senior editor, who saw the value in the James family's story and the need to share it with a broader audience. I also express my gratitude to Thomas Bedenbaugh, Valerie Burton, Iris Levesque, Alyssa Brown, Elizabeth Orange, Madge Duffey, and Lindsay Starr for their support, assistance, and quality of work. Additionally, I wish to thank Michelle Witkowski and Joyce Li at Westchester Publishing Services for their helpful suggestions and comments. I also owe a special gratitude to Jessica Ryan for carefully proofreading the page proofs; her helpful suggestions were invaluable.

Ascension

# Prologue

The sun rolled high in the sapphire sky the morning of May 18, 2019, as Samuel James, his wife, Valerie, son Gabriel, daughter Senya, and I breezed along the marshy coastal region of Highway 17 en route to Elizabeth City, North Carolina, to celebrate his brother Wayne's retirement. Nearly nineteen months had passed since my chance meeting with Samuel at NASA, and much had occurred in the intervening months. I was in the process of writing the James family's story based on telephone interviews as a result of our serendipitous encounter. Three weeks earlier, I had shared a draft copy of several chapters with the siblings so I could digest their feedback. At the celebration, I eagerly anticipated meeting family for the first time—all Samuel's eleven siblings and the matriarch, Pennie—and there, hopefully, I would get a multifaceted accounting of their collective story. Having steeped myself deeply inside with their words, thoughts, and valence of emotions for well over a year, I experienced and truly felt, at times, an intimate kindred connection with the family. Still, I wondered what it would be like to meet them in person. At such a thought, exhilaration and pensiveness gripped me, sporadically spiked with disquieted moments. Like a full-throttled engine, my active mind kicked into full gear and began dashing down the winding river of dry asphalt through the flatlands of the Great Dismal Swamp that stretched from southeastern Virginia to the northeastern borders of North Carolina. The viscosity of thought clumped together as dense as the trees of bald cypress, clogged with black gum, maple, Atlantic white cedar, and pine that flanked the highway, along with the endless wooden utility poles. Gliding along past this coastal countryside, my musings were broken only by the delight of small talk, by the sight of an old, rustic barn, a cluster of windmills, large tracts of potato farms, or by the ever encroachment of residential and commercial developments that sprang up along the roadside that lay before us. Undoubtedly, at the source of my internal push and pull was the larger question, did I get their story right?

Getting the story right is important to me, perhaps even an obsession over the long course of conducting interpretative research based on in-depth personal interviews and ethnographic fieldwork. Its meaning became abundantly clear about four years prior when I was interviewed for a newsletter.

Upon reading the printed story, the quotes attributed to me were somewhat akin to being switched at birth. For me, this incident raised not only significant questions about the process of listening, hearing, and interpreting but also about the mental and physical state of the interviewer. How is a message communicated and received? Who is the sender? Who is the receiver? How does one encode or decode a message? Do we listen, hear, and interpret through the prism of age, class, race, gender, culture, or other attributes? What is the impact of intensity, pitch, tone, and sentence accentuation in listening, hearing, and interpreting? And more important, what is the significance of nonverbal behavior in the communication process? Psychologist Albert Mehrabian, noting the importance of verbal and nonverbal communication in putting forward a message concerning feelings and attitudes, concluded in his experimental study that words accounted for only 7 percent of the message, tone of voice accounted for 38 percent, and body language accounted for 55 percent.[1]

Had I listened, heard, and interpreted their family narrative suitably for all the siblings? To some extent, Samuel relieved some of my misgivings when he said, "Lois, I thought you had babysat for us. It was like you were there with us." Mary claimed that she was still in the tree, the one she would climb while awaiting her father's return from work. "You made my father come alive again," she merrily declared. The evening prior to meeting everyone in person, Debbie, Karen, and Samuel sent what I considered relatively minor corrections and modifications that slightly eased my mind. This easement was tempered, however, by Terri's chastening reminder: "As amazing as you are, Dr. Benjamin, you are not perfect." "Baby Girl" had noted a possible gaffe and indicated that she would consult with Lubertha for its accuracy. However, upon our arrival at Northeastern High School, a venue brimming with heartfelt, memorable moments of the siblings' school life, all reservations ceased after meeting Debbie. As the first to greet me, her warm welcome layered me, like a Hawaiian lei, with the sweet scent of hospitality. It was a balm for the soul that calmed a restive spirit.

Roscoe Jr. was not in attendance at the celebration since he was officiating at an out-of-state wedding. Nonetheless, when I was introduced to the other siblings—Lubertha, Mary, Darlene, Karen, Shirley, Wayne, Beverly, Terri, and Eric, along with their mother, Pennie, they wrapped their loving arms of kindness around my shoulders and extended a warm security blanket. Henri Nouwen, a Dutch Catholic priest, believes "true hospitality is welcoming the stranger on her own terms. This kind of hospitality can only be offered by those who've found the center of their lives in their own hearts." I can bear witness that hospitality along with compassion, helpfulness, and respect are at the epicenter of their ideals and actions, some of the many important building blocks that create strong, caring individuals, families, and communities.

Such hospitality was on full display at Wayne's retirement celebration. In particular, it was evident that Wayne had transported such noble character traits from his building block of familial generosity, along with other values and skills, to build a caring community of learners and citizens at Northeastern High School. Family, friends, colleagues, staff, and people from the community gathered at its football stadium to celebrate and pay tribute to his twenty-eight years of dedicated teaching and service at Northeastern High School. Twenty-eight banners lined the football field, representing each year as the director of the band. It was the same venue where he performed as a student. To Wayne's surprise, seventy-five of his students, as well as alumni of Northeastern High School, were there for the celebration. Some had traveled great distances from across the contiguous United States, and others journeyed as far away as Alaska, Guam, and Saipan. At the sight of seeing his former students who returned to acknowledge his contribution to their lives, he was so overcome with emotion that he wept: his body quivered as he buried his face in his tear-stained handkerchief. Colleagues, staff, and especially students spoke glowingly of his positive impact at Northeastern High School. I spoke with David Albert, the former band director at Northeastern High School, who recalled an event that required him to be away from the school during Wayne's senior year as a band member, so he left Wayne in charge of the junior band. When he returned, the band had remarkably improved under Wayne's tutelage. At that point, the teacher knew his pupil had something special, the cosmic factor.

Wayne's galactic gift included his compassion and passion to motivate students to live beyond themselves, to push them toward excellence, and to empower and inspire them to do their best. I spoke with four of his former students who validated Henry Adams's prominent maxim, "A teacher affects eternity; he can never tell where his influence stops." Two young men, one who resided in Ohio and the other in Alaska, claimed that prior to their encounter with "Mr. James, we were nitwits and knuckleheads." Both noted that he taught them to value themselves, while encouraging and promoting positive masculinity. The young man living in Ohio graduated from Ohio State University and worked as a pharmacist technician. Another young man stated that he was reared by his single-parent mother, and "Mr. James served as an important father figure." A young woman who taught school in the vicinity of Elizabeth City was so effusive in her praise of "Mr. James" that she wondered, like the other three, "without his influence, what would have become of me?" Not present at the gathering were two of his former band members residing in Sydney, Australia. They invited him to perform with the Sydney Symphony Orchestra, a dream that came true in July 2019. With that request, the building block of Wayne's familial arms of kindness extended into the international arena, helping to build caring communities beyond borders.

After Wayne's festive fete ended, family assembled at the James family home, the one built by their father, Roscoe. Authentic detailed displays of loving kindness, acceptance, openness, and compassion toward others, one another, and toward me were omnipresent at every nook and cranny and were expressed in infinite ways. For instance, when Samuel had a minor problem starting his vehicle when leaving the celebration, several family members stayed close by until the problem was resolved. Terri texted Mary, making certain that she had not left, adding, "Mary can fix anything." Upon arrival at their home, the cheery ambience was engaging and relaxing. The scent of serenity swayed and swirled in the air, anointing spaces with acceptance of individual needs and differences. Family members engaged in spirited talk, while warmly greeting and embracing one another. As they gathered in the family room, I glanced at the collection of portraits that hung on the wall. One in particular had a striking resemblance to a snapshot of Roscoe Sr. that Eric had sent me, and I requested to have a closer view. When Darlene joined me, she identified the persons in the photograph as Roscoe's father and mother. I asked questions and gathered additional data about the family. One inquiry was about Roscoe's work as a plasterer. With that probe, Darlene graciously directed my attention toward Roscoe's fine craftsmanship of artistic plastering that adorned the dining room and living room walls and ceilings, the latter had been recently restored by Roscoe Jr. I sat for a while in their elegant living room, filled with antiques collected by Pennie, talking at various lengths with Lubertha, Debbie, Beverly, and Karen, who busied herself in the kitchen. Wayne greeted me in the parlor while making a brief appearance at home before heading to perform for another musical event scheduled at the annual North Carolina Potato Festival in Elizabeth City. Before departing, he reenacted an amusing, credible performance of the way his father would testify. Eventually, I returned to the family room where everyone was in full swing with music and jubilee. With Debbie on the piano and Eric on the trombone, they sang and played genres of popular and religious music. Debbie, Darlene, and others also danced. The performance culminated with a heartfelt rendition of Sister Sledge's 1979 hit song, "We Are Family." According to Lubertha, spending time with family is not only a means of bonding, but it also serves as a stress reducer, particularly for Eric, the baby boy. Effortlessly, family members appeared free to engage fully or partially in ongoing activities. For instance, Terri slept during some activities, while Pennie sat quietly and seemingly savored the memorable moments. In contrast, Beverly was a fully engaged participant in all the activities, expressing delight at seeing her brothers and sisters together again. Her demonstrative and ethereal innocence seemed joyful and laved with purity of heart.

Assuring me of the family's authenticity, Malissa, Eric's wife, sat next to me in the family room and whispered, "This is the way they are all the time. It is no act." When the time came for my departure, we lovingly hugged and said our goodbyes; however, before parting, Shirley had me account for all the siblings in birth order and by name at least twice. I also had to identify each by sight to make certain that I got everyone right. I am pleased that I passed Shirley's test. When I left the James family home that day, it took almost six months before I could articulate the experience with some clarity, but I knew something profound had happened.

Humor, loving acts of compassion, kindness, grace, and joy seemed as natural as breathing in the James family. Several studies support acts of kindness can have a rippling effect on others—that is, for both the receiver and the giver. Such acts enhance well-being, happiness, and joy and increase the desire to perform virtuous deeds. In essence, having positive emotions, life satisfaction, and prosocial behavior can help to broaden individuals' thought-action performances. Additionally, it can also increase their social and cultural capital.[2] Meeting the Jameses in person heightened my consciousness about kindness and its impact, leading to my conceptualization of two types of kindness: transcendent and transactional. Both have positive intentions and effects and can be reinforcing. However, the former is universal and enduring: it is unobligated or unexpected and emanates within an individual. In contrast, the latter is ordinary and transitory: it is obligated or expected and emanates outside an individual—that is, a pleasant service transaction or greeting. Call it kindness, compassion, empathy, hospitality, or by whatever name, it is perhaps the reason for New York City restauranteur Danny Meyer's belief that "hospitality is present when something happens for you. It is absent when something happens to you. Those two simple prepositions for and to express it all."

Possibly some element of truth exists in this adage because when I met the James family in person, something happened *for* me. What happened *for* me was an existential encounter with transcendent kindness, along with transactional kindness. With transcendent kindness, I was embraced into a community of nonjudgmental acceptance, compassion, love, humility, patience, understanding, and integrity. My vulnerabilities loosened after a lifetime of dancing to the rhythm of my own soul. The mask slackened, and the sometimes seemingly aloof self-presentation broke open and unmasked the warmth of my heart and the treasure of my kindness. I felt in my heart and I knew in my bones that I experienced oneness with myself, with the Jameses, and with others. Our souls melded and we danced in step to the rhythm. My thoughts and emotions felt no boundaries or no preoccupation with the past or future as I moved beyond the mundane bounds of ordinary human existence that drive basic needs and self-interests. Although my feelings and thoughts incorporated the five sensory experiences, they were beyond them. Such kindness is cosmic, unlike transactional kindness, which is conventional. The former is, indeed, a pivotal building block of the caring community or the "beloved community" as Martin Luther King Jr. described. This unfolding of higher consciousness is a knowing awareness or desire to discern transcendent values in ourselves and others and to live them unswervingly. To accept or reject transcendent values like kindness, compassion, humility, or unconditional love as an important part of a purposeful unfolding of life in our universe is for the seeker to answer. But what I can say is that my encounter with the Jameses was a transcendent experience and feeling. Some may call it by another name; I choose to call it spiritual. This way of knowing is more to understanding than logic or reasoning, for it is felt but not observed, thus cannot be accounted for scientifically.

My personal encounter was inseparable from what happened *for me* as a sociologist. In retrospect, my sociological eye focused on the core values that helped to shape the objective success of the James siblings. That is, for instance, what influences contributed to their educational attainment? Hence, I concentrated on such variables as faith, family, work ethic, strong belief in education, and their solid sense of empowerment, optimism, service, and respect for self and others in telling their story. I believed these values were key attributes that helped to explain their objective success and helped to build their social capital and strong family ties.

Admittedly, although I deeply admired the James family's noble character traits such as kindness, empathy, compassion, friendliness, humility, and generosity, I undervalued these emotional and transcendent qualities. But now I see these attributes as the subjective underbelly of success in contributing to their family's strengths and solidarity. Like most in the world of academe, my sociological eye had blind spots regarding the importance of these ascendant qualities. On the contrary, transactional kindness, couched in the jargon of collegiality, is a purported ideal norm in academe, although too often not its reality. Accordingly, in the academy, transcendent kindness can be underappreciated since it is viewed as being at the expense of fostering critical thinking and constructive critiquing, even if sometimes scholars are excoriating, demeaning, diminishing, dismissing, and not so constructive in their criticisms. Perhaps this way of thinking results from the false dichotomy that exists between emotion and intellect, especially since kindness is associated with emotion and intellect with ideas. In fact, kindness, empathy, and caring are too often deemed as a weakness and not as a strength. This is especially the case in the so-called merit-based system of academia, where promotion and tenure are based on the criteria of research, teaching, and service. Such acquisition of rank and status is a scarce commodity, especially in the present climate, where higher education is viewed through the lens of a business model. In such an individualistic and competitive climate, it is not surprising to find a paucity of studies about transcendent kindness. Perhaps it is a reflection of the larger societal organizing principles, social structure, and social interactions that so often regard transcendent kindness as too moralistic and sentimental. Underlying this belief is a perception of the world as a place of scarcity instead of abundance. This Hobbesian worldview, which grew out of the sixteenth century, maintains that humans are selfish and brutish. The documentary research quickly confirms a plethora of scholarly works on societal maladies and its relations to power, class, gender, race, and culture as opposed to societal strengths. Refreshingly, however, an upsurge of studies within the last decade, though still relatively scant, has focused on kindness, as well as compassion, empathy, and generosity in the field of positive psychology. Except for a few studies, sociology, as well as other disciplines in the social sciences, has not followed, for whatever reason, the lead of positive psychology. Perhaps it is, as previously noted, the result of binary thinking rooted in the Enlightenment era, which suggests that kindness and other transcendent traits are deemed too quixotic or relational. On the contrary, the focus on class and power is seen as observable and rational.

Thus, it stands to reason that in doing social research based on the scientific method, the focus is on objectivity and being value-free. Hence, researchers are expected to remain aloof from the individuals they study.

Note the way the researcher describes people who are being studied as subjects, respondents, interviewees, or participants, suggesting a hierarchal relationship. This stratification continues in the production of knowledge since the researcher has reign over what to include and what to exclude in the collection of data. The researcher also defines the problem, develops the social constructs and measurements, and analyzes and interprets findings without the input of the individuals being studied. With the empirical mode of thinking, which emphasizes the importance of objectivity and value neutrality, it is also essential to maintain proper distance between the researcher and subject to avoid contaminating the process of data collection and analysis. In interpretive research, even though researchers are more acutely aware of the shortcomings of social scientific research, they, in general, adhere to the scientific canon of avoiding becoming too close to the individuals being studied. Moreover, like the empiricists, the interpretivists commonly ignore the hierarchal relations inherent in the production of knowledge—that is, how people are studied, cataloged, and reported.

As a sociologist, I have followed both the empiricist and interpretive ways of doing sociology, while eagerly unearthing patterns and meanings in human behavior and empathetically understanding cultural contexts and social structures in which individuals and groups carry out those lives. Heretofore, in any research project, I had a purpose, a process, and a passion to discover patterns in human behavior that brought immense satisfaction until my next exploratory venture. Unequivocally, I love the process of doing sociology, so perhaps that is the unconscious reason for blurting out to Samuel James, "I want to interview you" upon hearing snippets of his family story on that memorable day of October 21, 2017. However, unlike previous projects, this undertaking was absent of purpose, process, or passion. I had only an elusive yearning to understand patterns of their objective success. Earlier in the research process, when I conducted my first family interview, Lubertha spoke these words:

> This visit is bigger than your encounter with Sam. You don't even
> know what you are doing right now. None of us do. But we all agree,
> we are not in control of this. God is in control. Ms. Lois, God bless you
> and wherever this leads. Our hope is that so many more can be helped
> by our story. This will bring so many more to Jesus Christ. All the glory
> belongs to Him. If the Lord doesn't get the glory out of this, our effort
> is in vain. But I do believe it is ordered by God. I believe He has
> ordered our steps to help somebody else, and He is using you as an

instrument to get this together for a greater cause. God bless your heart in Jesus's name.

The power of those words did not have the same meaning at the time she spoke them. I was further along in the process when Lubertha's words became abundantly clear. So without belaboring every corner and turn of this 99 percent labor of love and 1 percent labor of loathing, I can say this research jaunt with the Jameses has been a journey of the soul, where I embraced my spiritual awakenings and life's mysteries, my joyous mornings of divine light, my shadowy nights of soul cries, and my soul silence—all in their myriad shades of complexity and ambiguity. In my journey, I vacillated from sometimes doing sociology—that is, the focus on *what is*—to the sociology of being—that is, the focus of *what might be*—when I met the Jameses, especially when I encountered them in person. Prior to our acquaintance, my sociological gaze was always steady in the role of complete observer or observer as participant. With this venture, I crossed boundaries by all measures. I threw caution to the wind in terms of process and purpose: I embraced the people. Shedding my observer as participant facade, I did not heed the warning of becoming too close to the so-called subjects, participants, or respondents. I unabashedly "fell in love" not with the subjects but with the Jameses. I became a complete participant. The family's kind, open, compassionate, and nonjudgmental noble character was infectious, unobligated, and transcendent. The old adage, "When the student is ready, the teacher will appear" is applicable here. The James family became my teacher. I embraced my journey of the soul and the spiritual and humanistic dimension of this research.

Unwittingly, I had returned to the original intent of the forefather of sociology, Auguste Comte, the founder of positivism, a philosophical and religious movement.[3] His notion of positivism, unlike its present usage, does not separate the philosophy of science from political philosophy. Comte's primary goal was to reorganize society, and his aim was to employ science in achieving that end. Sociologists like Karl Marx, Lester Ward, Albion Small, W. E. B. Du Bois, Pitirim A. Sorokin, Ernest Becker, and R. Dean Wright, who were in the tradition of Comte, also saw sociology as a way to improve society. By the second half of the twentieth century, however, scientific positivism had become fully ensconced as the dominant model in the discipline of sociology. William Du Bois and R. Dean Wright find this move to science a curious happening. "Science was not seen as a human act but was simply viewed as a neutral, objective process. We pretend that the scientific act of looking isn't a part of human behavior: the world just *appears* before our lenses. We refuse to pay any attention to our act of viewing (what is going on 'In Here') and pretend we are just objectively seeing the 'Out There.' As we move from physical science to social science, we then turn our objective scientific lenses back upon ourselves to view human behavior. You can't refuse to acknowledge that science is a human act and then utilize our constructed mechanical science to understand the human. We can't decide to view the 'Out There' by denying the 'In Here' and then turn around and use such a method to do the 'In Here.'"[4]

Although Du Bois and Wright reveal the illogicalness of this assumption, they reiterate that it is what a human science that employs only the scientific method does. It objectifies people. During the counterrevolutionary movement of the 1960s and 1970s, sociologists like John Glass, in *Toward a Sociology of Being: The Humanistic Potential*, reacted to scientific positivism and its objectification of humans.[5] Glass and likeminded sociologists believed that as a human science, sociology focused too much on the status quo, on what is at the expense of what might be. Hence, he, along with other humanistic sociologists, called for a radical paradigmatic shift in the pessimistic image of human, society, science, and the sociological undertaking.

Glass's way of thinking was in tandem with Ernest A. Becker who saw two competing sociologies: The first one is "the superordinate science of humanity which calls us to action and to change the world. It is an ideal science concerned with not just what is but what ought to be. . . . The second sociology is the narrow academic discipline content to color within the lines and seek only journal articles, research grants, and tenure."[6] Since Becker and Glass believed that the aim of the discipline is to make life better, they advocated for a humanistic approach to the study of sociology. This meant challenging and engaging scholars in the field of sociology to study institutions, cultural and social structures, and values that facilitate the development of individuals and enrich them to make autonomous and responsible choices.

In contrast to the humanistic perspective, which values people as ends in themselves, the scientific approach too often views people as objects or means. Du Bois and Wright argue, "Our means and ends must correlate. Science would simply tack values on at the end of what otherwise was a scientific process. Humanism would begin with values and human purposes. Scientific knowledge views the human as separate and just an object of study. Humanism sees the human as intimately intertwined in the whole process of consciousness and knowing."[7]

In seeing the human as knitted into the "whole process of consciousness and knowing," perhaps folk sociology, which Howard Odum defined "as a basic subject field for the historical study of total human society in process and for the empirical study of group behavior in interaction,"[8] can also find a home in humanism, or in knitters' terminology, become at minimum a lifesaver. Whether it is folk sociology, scientific sociology, humanistic sociology, in addition to other perspectives, each offers a heuristic framework for conceptualizing and understanding the social world. However, a critical stance of each perspective is called for at all times. The reason being that in the sociological family tree, each branch of knowledge can produce beneficial fruit and simultaneously have some nocuous side effects. It depends on how each perspective frames its epistemology—that is, its way of knowing. Basically, each arrives at assumptions about the social world by asking such epistemological questions as, What is knowledge? Can we have knowledge? What do people know? How do we get knowledge? What are the many ways of knowing? What are the necessary and appropriate conditions of knowledge? What is the configuration of knowledge? What are its limitations? What causal hypothesis do people have about how things operate? How do people construct their plans and actions around these frameworks? How each philosophical orientation perceives these questions impact worldview, theoretical and methodological assumptions, beliefs, values, norms, and behaviors.

Is there a way out of this binary thinking—the dilemma of forcing sociologists to choose one epistemological framework over another? When a critical stance is employed, perhaps we can visualize a knitting of frameworks or perhaps, at best, an interlacing peaceful coexistence of doing sociology with the sociology of being to reenvision C. Wright Mills's notion of the sociological imagination that not only connects the individual's private and public sphere but also embraces the fruitful and beneficial insights of humanistic sociology, scientific sociology, as well as folk sociology while debunking unfavorable side effects. I take this multipronged approach in studying the James family. Such a path to knowledge appears promising since it encourages multiple ways of seeing and also enhances a higher level of consciousness that may well contribute to improving society. Think of commercial farmers as being somewhat analogous to social scientific sociologists in this way. The former grows produce to sell at the market for profit, while the latter produces knowledge for knowledge's sake, or for a better understanding of how society works, or to receive tenure or promotion. When commercial farmers produce more food than people are willing to buy, not only are they practicing unsustainable land management, but too often, they plough over their crops and allow them to lay waste or rot in fields when they are unable to sell them

them because of market conditions. Likewise, scientific sociologists produce knowledge that is more concerned with findings and explanations of social issues and phenomena than they are with their applications; hence, this accumulation of knowledge too frequently lies unread on library shelves or in digital archives. Instead of permitting produce rots in the fields or knowledge lies fallow on library shelves, humanistic sociologists reimagine a way to distribute those crops to people who are food insecure. In a similar vein, they look at how to apply the knowledge of social scientific sociologists to make society more just, fair, and equitable through social action.

Here, I return to transcendent and transactional kindness, a trait of the James family's noble character, one of the nine core values that make up their value system. I might add one that transformed my own thinking about the sociology of doing and sociology of being when I met the family. Their everyday acts of kindness emerged from a family value system that advocates everyone should be treated equally regardless of circumstances, and it is grounded in their Christian faith. I found their noble character consisting of such traits as kindness, love, humility, care ethic, fairness, and honesty to be contagious. Families and societies have a major influence on values, which are rudimentary and important beliefs that guide or motivate attitudes or actions of individuals, groups, institutions, and societies. They help us to determine what is important and worthwhile to us and how we behave toward others. In addition, they help us to describe the kind of person we desire to be with ourselves and in our interaction with others. Values matter; therefore, they are worthy of being studied. A review of the literature,[9] however, suggests otherwise, regarding the paucity of research on how values matter in daily living and decision makings. Perhaps, this is due in part to the difficulty in measuring values and in part to the lack of data of what values may do. Could it be because sociologists rarely write about what should be valued? Instead, they describe differences in values, depict shared values among groups and societies, and elucidate their origins and consequences. In my research and interaction with the James family and their value system, I concur with the standpoint of humanistic sociology that values should not only be studied, but if they also promote the enhancement of individuals, groups, and societies, they should be advocated. Transcendent kindness, for example, matters. And what values matter is a central question of humanistic sociology.

> If humanistic sociology is to make values matter in designing the
> world, we must ask: Which values? The sociologists should not strive

to be without values. Cultural relativity means taking your values off long enough to see. It does not mean to be without values. Objectivity means putting things in perspective. It really means honesty—not to falsify things. The core element of objectivity is "respect." Respect, according to Eric Fromm, is from the original root meaning "to look at." We must bring our values to work. Humanism is not a hobby we do after work: making a better world must be the real work of sociology.[10]

The story of the James family can become a little leap in the holy grail of humanists to make a better and more peaceful world order. In Confucius's understanding of world order, the goal is "ping,"[11] denoting peace, harmony, equity, and fairness. To that end, Confucius postulated, "To put the world in order, we must first put the nation in order; to put the nation in order, we must first put the family in order; to put the family in order, we must first cultivate our personal life; to cultivate our personal life, we must first set our hearts right."

## CHAPTER ONE

# A Curious Chance Encounter

## *A Social Explorer Meets a NASA STEM Problem Solver*

Space exploration captivates me because of its scientific importance and its significance for the future of humanity. On a sunlit Saturday, October 21, 2017, this fascination propelled me to the NASA Langley Research Center for its hundredth-anniversary celebration in Hampton, Virginia. But so did a déjà vu phenomenon, a sense that some unexpected happening would alter my life. My long-held allure for space and aeronautics stemmed from my youthful wonder at watching the launch of the first American, Alan Shepard, into space aboard the Mercury-Redstone rocket to hearing President John F. Kennedy boldly pledge to put a man on the moon, to seeing Neil Armstrong land on its surface a few years later. As an African American woman, this centennial celebration was especially triumphant as NASA Langley had been prominently featured in the Academy Award–nominated film *Hidden Figures*, which chronicles the journeys of several local African American pioneers in space exploration as the nation journeyed toward civil rights. While I wielded my camera as a social explorer toward the inner workings of society, I had always admired scientists and engineers who pointed their own at the stars.

As I toured the displays of wind tunnels and thought of human space travels, my eyes caught a tall, distinguished-looking gentleman who was holding a fabricated model aircraft as he passionately explained its design to an onlooker. He was the only African American exhibitor in the spacious room.

I paused for a moment to watch. To the untrained eye, that would not be cause for pause, but for African Americans, especially those of us who remember the struggle to integrate such spaces, we are intuitively conditioned to taking inventory of how many people look like us in such venues.

Simultaneously, my thoughts for that moment turned to my next exhibit in a proximate venue, the *Hidden Figures* exhibit, and I wondered if he might have been missed. I, along with my guests, sauntered over to his table and waited patiently for him to conclude his spiel with the bystander. When my turn came, I peppered him with questions about his project and learned of his thirty-year career and numerous accomplishments at NASA Langley, which included the Exceptional Service Medal in 2004. He also had two co-patents at NASA—a curved weaving loom and a pressure-assisted linear seal in an inflatable airlock. Samuel James, as I later learned his name, was a mechanical engineering technician in the Aerospace Composite Models Development. I asked about his family. A flood of pride arose in him as he talked of his upbringing in the small town of Elizabeth City, North Carolina, a population of 17,905.

He spoke about his father, Roscoe James, and offered, "He was a man of character. I always idolized my daddy, and he became my role model. I always said that I wanted to grow up and be like my father." His mother, Pennie, also towered over his life. At times, she was a disciplinarian; at times, she was a softer nurturer. She also taught him how to be tough. I learned a few more tidbits about Samuel. He was one of twelve children. He was devoutly religious. I also learned later, to my surprise, that despite the confidence and charisma he displayed speaking in front of the rapt audience for the NASA event, at one time in his life, he shirked from the spotlight.

A plethora of unspoken questions jogged through my mind. I was vacillating between yielding to the pilot light of my inner curiosity and yet constrained by my duty-bound value of not starting something without committing full scale. I strained to hold the questions welling inside me at bay. But the more Samuel spoke, the more they brimmed over. Part of me hoped Samuel's story in the exhibit hall would veer off into familiar directions or cease to open thought-provoking treasure trails of data. The abatement never came. I was being reeled in.

What builds a man like Samuel James?

Oftentimes, individuals of great professional acumen ascribe to a self-made narrative. This is welded to American character with the at times idolatry of individualism. Yet, here Samuel James stood, at the pinnacle of his success, in the height of American innovation professing the virtues and education he received from the most humble of roots. To explain his success in a profession that dealt in science and empirical facts, Samuel James credited his faith. He credited his father, a man who left school in the seventh grade, as the source of the considerable intellect he now wielded. He set the first few crumbs on the trail. I could not bring myself to veer off the path he was leading me toward. And although he was a man of great achievement, Samuel James tempered his successes with humility. "We treat everyone the same, from the billionaire to the homeless," he would later tell me.

What helped Samuel James rise from the small town in North Carolina? What about his family? What were their life chances? What were their struggles? What forged their journey forward?

I would learn Samuel possessed a relentless curiosity that welled inside of him. He was also exceptionally creative. But his curiosity and creativity were bonded to an even harder character trait that so often eludes individuals who have the former gifts. At the base of Samuel's creativity and curiosity was discipline. But his was a self-discipline, the ability to push himself forward, to remain motivated, and take control despite his emotional or physical state of being. This trait allowed him to not only dream of the "what might be," but it also allowed him to bring his creative ideas into reality. It took a while to pick up the habits he developed over time.

Consider his daily routine.

Each morning, before all else, he maintained his spirituality. "The first thing I do when I wake up is to get on my knees," he said. After morning prayers, as he ate his usual breakfast of oatmeal fortified with antioxidant-rich blueberries or strawberries, he also reviewed notes in his journal. At Sunday services during the weekend, he took meticulous notes, noting biblical passages referenced by his pastor for further personal study. He also read the journal alongside his Bible in the mornings during breakfast, scouring each page for more spiritual nourishment, and taking time to meditate on the lessons as he searched for applications he might build onto his daily walk with the Almighty.

In a sense, just as he was trained to treat all people the same, Samuel also viewed any chance to learn something new with the same vigor, whether it was spiritual, scientific, or even the recreational logic, such as the word puzzle books he kept in his house. In the morning, whenever possible, he also made time to stop by his garage, which functions as a makeshift scientific laboratory for him.

Samuel tinkered with different projects, two of which he had secured patents, as noted, and yet, he still made sure he had enough time to arrive at his job at NASA not only punctually but early for the day's work. "I'm a dependable person," Samuel assured me. "When somebody gives me a time, if I don't do it on time, it bothers me." Each task for the day was attacked with zeal, each project was a new frontier, an opportunity to explore and interact and problem solve and experience something yet unknown. He could turn anything into an adventure, whether it was a trip to church or a day's work building a path to the stars.

Despite what I had learned later about Samuel, intuitively, I knew from my initial encounter, he had a good story, one that my own insatiable curiosity would not be able to walk away from without hearing. It was not the simple, casual storytelling one might exchange in polite company or relay over a cup of tea. This one would take work and vigor to hear and understand. It would take cumbersome effort to sort beneath the surface into the deeper chambers. A man like Samuel James did not happen by accident. And like any story, other narratives and characters emerged that enriched his own. To understand Samuel, one had to understand his eleven siblings and the journeys they took, the way they influenced him, the identity they collectively formed that was stronger than any one strand of individuality. I sensed an untold story was behind his life crying out to be heard. The irony of this chance encounter was that Samuel and I nearly missed each other. Whereas I woke up excited for the day of NASA exploration, I would later learn Samuel was contemplating a rare day off. He gets a steady stream of requests each year for different speaking engagements for NASA and this day was an optional activity. He woke up that October morning thinking he would rest and get ahead on other, more pressing tasks. But being a man of dedication and commitment, he decided to show up at the exhibit, nonetheless, speaking with full enthusiasm and excitement about the work he did for the space agency. Before I had a chance to monitor my thoughts, I blurted out, "I would like to interview you."

As soon as those words slipped my lips, a quandary began. "What have I done to myself?" I asked. I was basking in my liberated schedule after spending thirty-four years in the ivory tower. Upon retiring, I declared I would not write another academic book, certainly not one involving descriptive, exploratory qualitative research. How time-consuming to observe human behaviors, their intricacies and nuances, while peeling back the layers to see what social bonds and life experiences form the exteriors they present. It requires being fully present and immersed in the moment. It also necessitates some fine-tuning to hear the instruments that forge the voice that speaks to you. In time during the course of research, you forge your own instrument, a long-range lens camera of sorts to see past the outward layers and manifestations of people into the roots that produce them. This requires an insatiable, at times ill-timed penchant for curiosity and travel. It entails questioning and deep probing and listening and understanding from the person's perspective, which demands a deep reservoir of patience. It also requires note-taking, taping, and transcribing. I had gladly laid aside these tools honed over many decades and picked up my garden tools.

The only long-term project I had intentions on entangling myself in during this liberated phase of my life was the flower beds that lined my backyard. And I wanted to quench my lifelong curiosity for topics that had bypassed me as I dedicated myself to my research and students. Yet, Sheila

Stevens, my closest and longtime friend from our days at the University of California, Berkeley, as the first two Black women who entered its graduate program in the Department of Sociology, had chided me when I boasted about my leisurely retirement plans, saying, "You're always going to be a sociologist, no matter what." I scoffed at the notion.

Sheila is often right.

But like the prophets whose word went unheeded in Scripture, I inevitably saw the truth all too late in Sheila's words. Against all odds, I soon found myself immersed in the story of Samuel James's family.

The family that built Samuel James gave me new understanding, not only of the field I had dedicated a lifetime of work but also a new understanding of myself.

Consequences are inevitable for every decision. Sometimes they work against you. Sometimes they work in your favor. This decision put me on a journey that was unlike any other during my career. I had to accept the consequences.

It took me outside of the halls of the most elite academia, beyond the layers of sociological literature and theoretical thoughts that lie in my mind, to a place that landed squarely outside of my comfort zone. What began as another inquiry into the studies to which I had become so accustomed became an immersive experience that broke new ground in the studies I spent my life pursuing. I broke my rules. I learned new ways to learn. I learned that sometimes a study cannot be done from a space of detachment. Sometimes to tell a story, one has to lean into the warmth of the storytellers. One accepts the tactile feelings that come with it. Instead of repressing the charm of the family I met, I embraced them.

My life and work had taken me from the red-clay soil and tall pines of Georgia to the sandy soil and redwood trees of California. I had traveled overseas, conducting research in rural villages and teeming cities in eleven countries on the African continent and in Haiti and Jamaica. My odyssey with the James family brought me to a new place, one I suspect I had spent a lifetime searching for: "home." To learn their story, to understand their home, I had to start with the first person Samuel mentioned to me, his father, Roscoe James.

## CHAPTER TWO

# Roscoe James

*Dreaming the Legacy of a Good Name*

The scent of pine hung heavily around the towering copse of trees that graced the childhood farmette of Roscoe James in Woodville, North Carolina. Its aroma comingled with the malodorous barnyard whiffs of chicken, cows, goats, and pigs that wafted through the air. This rivalrous emanation engulfed his nares, as he sat on a rustic stump beneath the grove and dutifully watched, like a shepherd boy, over the herd of cows and goats grazing in flat, verdant meadows owned by his parents, Eula and Tommy James. Perhaps the contending smell of pine, known in folklore tradition for its magical and medicinal makings, calmed and elevated his inner being. With a renewed sense of energy, the spirited lad gazed over the landscape that day in 1948, merely three years after the end of World War II, and reflected on his coming of age. Imaginably, he envisioned his future and wondered, what were the life chances of a fourteen-year-old African American male who was born and bred in Woodville, North Carolina, a rural hamlet near Elizabeth City? De jure segregation in the South was the order of the day when he was born in 1934 amid the Great Depression, and it remained so in 1948. Additionally, most Blacks were still employed in the low-paying service sector of the economy. Even though this pattern began to change after the war, the chances of Roscoe continuing his life as a farmer, digging potatoes, picking cabbages, and tending goats or joining the ranks of unskilled laborers in his family and community were highly probable, especially since his education was hampered. Farm duties and responsibilities were calling him; hence, his father had forced Roscoe, along with his brothers, to forsake school in the seventh grade. Despite the growth of universal education and the passage of child labor laws in the early twentieth century, such practices were not diffused uniformly in America. Consequently, early school dropout was customary during that era, especially in the rural South where many hands were needed for farm life. Moreover, the concept of adolescence, popularized by G. Stanley Hall, president of the American Psychological Association in the early twentieth century, had not fully taken hold for individuals like Roscoe James and their families of orientation.[1] For such families, the transition between childhood and adulthood was brief. Hence, parents, like those of the nineteenth century, advised youth to assume adult responsibilities during the major shift from an agrarian to an industrial society.

Standing at six feet five inches, small wonder that Roscoe's blossoming manhood reminded him of coming adult responsibilities as a breadwinner, husband, and father, while gazing across the farm's grassland and watching over the flock blithely grazing. Despite his limited probabilities of upward social mobility, the eternal optimist and "visionary," as described by his son Samuel James, believed in unlimited possibilities. He dared to imagine the opportunity of owning land and being self-employed. With that vision and his deep and abiding religious faith, he cast his lot into the hands of God and set about to make it happen. His awakened manhood also stirred his longing for family. Born into a clan of twelve children, the pious lad prayed for twelve children that day while sitting under the pines. And undoubtedly, he pined for Pennie, the object of his affection, whom he hoped to someday marry and to bear his twelve children to carry on his "good name."

Remarkably, Roscoe and Pennie had known each other since childhood, having met in primary school around six years of age. During their daily three-mile school bus trips together, Roscoe had taken a liking to her. But it was not love at first sight for Pennie. He grew on her, and eventually, she became fond of him, noting that "he was kind and loved the Lord." He was also "a good provider and an honest man of his word who kept to himself." Since their families were interconnected, it helped, too, that her mother adored him and that Roscoe and her youngest brother George were friends. Likewise, both families were rooted strongly in the church; Roscoe sang in the choir and Pennie played the piano. With their families' blessings, seemingly at an early age, they were solemnly betrothed to each other.

When Roscoe left school, he no longer saw Pennie on a regular basis. Long hours of predawn risings, nightfall callings, and weekend shifts of dairy farming duties and other farm responsibilities intervened. Later, as he and his brothers grew older, they worked at a local construction company to assist the family. There, he became an apprentice, where he learned the craft of framing and drywalling houses. Although Roscoe had savored his long school bus rides with Pennie, whom he dearly missed, he was unperturbed by the separation. The strong-minded young man initiated a way to connect with Pennie since he needed to show his love for her during intermittent absences. Thus, Roscoe's sister Jennie V., who rode the school bus daily with Pennie, became the conduit to the paramours' hearts. Through her, he sent messages and money to his prospective mate. Undoubtedly, it was Roscoe's way of showing his commitment toward investing for a lifetime with Pennie.

Four years after Roscoe prayed for twelve children, the time for matrimony came shortly after Pennie's graduation from high school. In 1952, Roscoe and Pennie, at ages eighteen and nineteen, respectively, cast their net deep in spiritual waters of the sacrament of marriage and set their sails to the winds, knowing they could not direct the winds, but they could alter the sails. Afterward, the newly wedded shipmates tied the knot and dropped their anchor in Elizabeth City, North Carolina, and began building their family. Interestingly, Roscoe never told Pennie, whose parents had thirteen children, about his prayer for a dozen offspring. However, once their first ten came in the following chronological birth order—Lubertha, Debbie, Mary, Roscoe Jr., Darlene, Karen, Shirley, Samuel, Wayne, and Beverly—she accepted each child as "God's will." After their eleventh one, Terri, was "offered up to the Lord," Pennie remembered the bishop of their church announced, "One more, Roscoe." When Eric arrived, their twelfth child, he was designated the "miracle baby" since he languished at birth from spinal meningitis. Yet, he fought valiantly and overpowered it. Roscoe was grateful for Eric's survival, especially since the doctor had voiced bluntly to Roscoe and Pennie that "nothing further could be done for him. It was only a matter of time before he would leave this earth." But Roscoe declared emphatically, "No! I prayed for twelve, and he is going to be fine." And exultingly, he called all twelve children—eight daughters and four sons—his blessings. For Lubertha, their father's prayer for twelve children was a strong connection to "God keeping His word and delivering His promise," particularly since Pennie had three miscarriages. Still, as she pronounced, "The Lord allowed his twelve children to live."

When people inquired about Roscoe's large family, he exclaimed joyfully that it was "cheaper by the dozen," although it was sometimes a challenge to feed, clothe, and shelter twelve children. But Roscoe and Pennie were undaunted. They were enterprising and self-sufficient, so their children's needs were always met but not necessarily their wants. They were hardworking and as resilient as the yellow lotus flower rising from the murky, coastal ponds and lakes of North Carolina.

Like most women prior to the feminist movement of the 1960s, Pennie was primarily the home manager and chief nurturer of the children. But she also worked as the children grew older. She held odd jobs as a housekeeper and also worked for a few years at a thrift shop to supplement the family income. Her firstborn, Lubertha, who aided in childcare and household chores, made it feasible for her to work outside the home. With Pennie's supplemental family income, she purchased clothing at an immense savings to the family while employed at the shop. She also worked in an antique shop, where she taught herself to identify Depression glass and furniture at antique auction facilities. Eventually, the diligent and strong-willed Pennie opened her own antique shop. Pennie also earned a certificate in cosmetology.

Similarly, Roscoe, the chief breadwinner, also shared the entrepreneurial spirit with his mate. After working for a construction company and perfecting his trade, he preferred being at the helm of his business as a self-employed contractor. Sometimes, working as an independent plasterer and drywaller took him away from home for extended periods, as he contracted for jobs, occasionally for major companies, along the East Coast of the United States from Florida to Maine. To minimize his work travels, once he took five years off the road and opened a convenience store, which the older children ran when he resumed his work travels. Additionally, he had a mobile food truck that served the community. His hard work paid off. He saved enough money to buy land and to build the family's first home without a blueprint. Later when the family outgrew their first one, he built the second home also without a blueprint.

In precisely the same way Roscoe did not have a blueprint for building a house, he and Pennie did not have a design for building a family. As Samuel aptly pointed out, "Mother and Daddy did not have a blueprint on how to raise children. They did it as they went along. But they created their own blueprint." Despite nonexistent drawings, they still shared an undergirding framework. For Roscoe and Pennie, a spiritual reality bolstered their worldview. Perhaps it is best summed up in this way: people before things rather than things before people. Flowing from this perspective is a set of core values they shared with their children—beliefs that would become building blocks for a solid family. One of their paramount core values is faith. Lubertha, the oldest offspring, spoke passionately about their faith: "My parents grew up teaching us the values of learning who God is and who His Son is and this is our ultimate reason for living . . . and for me, that is the beauty of our family's foundation." They not only stressed the importance of faith but also "to be respectful to others, especially to older persons, and to help those that are less fortunate." Adding together their shared and individual values, Pennie and Roscoe collectively poured into their twelve children a solid foundation footer of nine core values: faith, family, noble character, respect, service, work ethic, empowerment, education, and optimism.

Unarguably, they framed their core values to raise successful children. All Pennie and Roscoe's children, except one—a daughter who is intellectually disabled—attended college and eight completed at least a bachelor's degree.

TABLE 2.1 Nine core values and the descriptors/indicators*

| Faith | Family | Noble character | Respect | Service | Work ethic | Empowerment | Education | Optimism |
|---|---|---|---|---|---|---|---|---|
| Heritage | Togetherness | Love | Civility | Helping others | Discipline | Resilience | High expectations | Joy |
| Faithful | Unity | Humility | Dignity of others | Sharing resources | Hard work | Can-do spirit | Parental engagement | Happy |
| God loving | Parental | Authenticity | Dignity of self | | Reliability | Agency | Home-school link | Laughter |
| Spiritual | Obedience | Compassion | Obedience to societal laws | | Optimism | Self-sufficiency | Expectation of college | Positive humor |
| Devotion to God | Shared values | Good name | | | Integrity | Self-efficacy | Value learning | Hope |
| Follow Jesus | | Generosity | | | Ambition | Resilience | Value excellence | Faith |
| Faith in God | | Trustworthiness | | | Dedication | Resourcefulness | High achievement | Positive outlook |
| Obedience to God | | Peace | | | Trustworthiness | Seize opportunities | | |
| God's will | | Reputation | | | Professionalism | Perseverance | | |
| Anointed | | Accountability | | | Conscientiousness | Sense of purpose | | |
| Highly blessed | | Patience | | | Responsibility | Tenacity | | |
| Family prayers | | Being the best | | | | | | |
| Devoutness | | Doing the best | | | | | | |
| Doers of the Word | | Care ethic | | | | | | |
| Christians | | Forgiveness | | | | | | |
| | | Gratitude | | | | | | |
| | | Nonjudgmental | | | | | | |
| | | Honest | | | | | | |
| | | Humility | | | | | | |

* The core values/descriptors are derived from the James family.

Except for Roscoe Jr., who incurred traffic fines and violations, none of the other children have ever been involved in the juvenile justice system or criminal justice system; nor have any been on public welfare assistance or in the foster care system. They are deeply immersed in their faith and community, and they are successful in the world of work. More important, members of the James family have maintained a high degree of generational solidarity among their clan.

What are the key ingredients in the recipe of Pennie and Roscoe James that produced this successful family in spite of a plethora of structural constraints? Roscoe and Pennie, in particular, were celebrated for their culinary feats. Her famous pound cake, chocolate layer cake, sweet potato pie, apple jacks, lemon meringue pie, barbecue chicken wings, salmon cakes, and collard greens were unparalleled, and so was his fried fish and fish roe, and his fried corn and corn fritters dripping in butter. Like the distinctive, blended ingredients of their home-cooked fare, they began in their test kitchen of child-rearing with a simple humble stew, which consisted of simmered faith in God and His Son Jesus Christ with family cohesiveness; they added heaping scoops of positive character traits—accountability, authenticity, civility, compassion, dignity, discipline, forgiveness, generosity, peace, respect for self and others, trustworthiness, and a potent pinch of patience. They sautéed together service, education, work ethic, can-do spirit, resourcefulness, being and doing the best with purpose, and stirred them in the stew. Last, Roscoe and Pennie topped the stew with a generous sprinkling of humor, joy, and love.

Whatever the instructional recipe, these fixings were baked, boiled, fried, poached, roasted, sautéed, or braised into their very being. Like the calibrated oven thermometer that produces consistency in outcome, Pennie and Roscoe calibrated their values and actions for consistency. Their offspring agreed unanimously, "They talked the talk and walked the walk."

Roscoe James died on December 15, 2000, but he continued to live in the souls of those he left behind. For indeed, the symbolic foundation of his life was faith, family, and community, as manifested in his sounds of joy, halos of hope, and seeds of service. His life was also a song and the people did the singing and praising. According to Samuel at his funeral service, "All the people came forward and told us how much he had helped them. He would get in his truck and go to other neighborhoods, and when he saw that other people could not afford his goods, he would give his goods away. He had a big heart. He purchased a used station wagon for a family of six or seven.

We did not find this out until he passed in 2000. We were not surprised since he was a giving person. He walked the walk and always tried to do God's will to the best of his ability."

Roscoe gave much of his time, talent, and money to "the least of these." Nonetheless, it was also his desire to bequeath to his twelve children a generous inheritance. But he would always remind them, "I cannot give you lots of money, but I can give you a good name." Simply put, French sociologist Pierre Bourdieu, writing in the late twentieth century, would have argued that Roscoe's desirable attribute-value system, defined as having a "good name," richly endowed his children in the form of social capital, essentially defined as nonmonetary resources.[2] It is those moral obligations and norms, social values—particularly trust—and resources connected with group membership and social networks that can have explicit benefits.

The bonding between children and parents based on shared values, parental norms, and mutual obligations in family relations is therefore a form of social capital. In itself, this intangible familial resource can be an influential source of power, having positive beneficial effects in terms of socioeconomic advantages, social well-being, social adjustment, cognition, and upward mobility.[3] With such celebratory pluses, the old proverbial saying about material wealth, "Shirtsleeves to shirtsleeves takes only three generations," can also be appropriated to intangible wealth. Like Roscoe's mornings of goading goats, the fruits of his loins are, too, prodded with field questions. For instance, how has Roscoe and Pennie James's social capital trust benefited their heirs? How have their beneficiaries leveraged their social capital creation to generate other forms of capital, such as cultural capital, the experience, education, skills, and knowledge that provide access to financial opportunities, or economic capital, the money and wealth that provide greater access to networks, goods, and resources? Is there a succession plan to pass on the family legacy to the third generation and beyond? In general, how can the family's bonding social capital be sustained across generations? First, to answer these and other questions that might arise, we can turn to the case narrative of Samuel James, the eighthborn child of Roscoe and Pennie James. Second, through collaborative dialogic lenses with the James siblings, we can witness how they are living their legacy, coauthoring their family history, and passing on their social capital. Third, in focusing on Roscoe and Pennie's grandchildren, we can grasp their continuities and challenges in sustaining social capital in the third generation. Fourth, in assessing the endowed social capital granted to the offspring of Pennie and

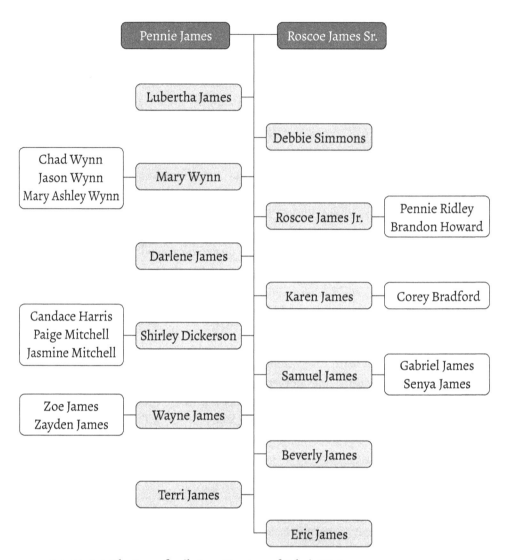

FIGURE 2.1 The James family tree. Courtesy of Valerie W. James.

Roscoe, we can look at outcomes in relation to worldview, leadership type, and social mobility. Finally, we can examine the larger implications of bonding social capital based on affirmative values for families, communities, the nation, and the world.

To help guide readers through the social excursions of the James family and how its individual members are connected, refer to the intergenerational family tree, found in figure 2.1.

CHAPTER THREE

# Samuel James
*Bearing the Good Name*

November 29, 2017, five weeks after my fortuitous meeting with Samuel James at NASA Langley Research Center, I held my initial interview with him. After our dialogue, Samuel gently inferred that his success could not be understood apart from his family. Hence, I undertook his wise nudging to heart, and thus my rich odyssey with the James family began. Instantaneously, I was bestowed a golden key that unlocked the James family's treasure chest of familial values and its contents of noble character.

I quickly unearthed a fundamental finding in the contents of their treasure chest—namely, the strong ties that bind the family. These familial links are essential building blocks in Samuel's success. And for this eighthborn and second son, success is not having "money or material things; rather, it is giving back and reaching out to the community, reaching out to youth and giving them guidance for a better life, and reaching out in life and caring and helping an individual in the community." Like die cast steel, Samuel's values were forged in the fire of faith and family. Service before self is only one of the deeply ingrained values that he extols. "Respect, commitment, trustworthiness, honesty, and fairness" are other high ideals he lauds, and they are personified within his faith.

Samuel breathed these ethics, and he witnessed the adherence of his parents to these ideals as they demonstrated them within the family, church, and community. A leader, and not a follower of the crowd, Samuel willingly shadowed in his parents' ethical footsteps. For instance, when Samuel was playing football on his college team at Elizabeth City State University, he recalled this incident: "Someone pulled out marijuana and started smoking. I told him to let me out of the car. I don't want to be around this. So many times, people have been in the wrong place at the wrong time. Although you were not smoking marijuana, it is on your clothes and the cops end up arresting you, too, and taking all of you to jail. I did not want to be a part of that scene. People would say that I dot my i's and cross my t's because I think about what my parents are saying and that is staying in my ears." Staying in Samuel's ears was his father's belief that marijuana, as well as other drugs, was "not good for you; it will take your life away." His father's wisdom,

"If you don't start nothing, it won't be nothing," also stayed in his ears. He noted, "I was the type of guy at an early age who did not follow the crowd. If I did not see it was right, I was not going with you. If you had guys who wanted to start a fight, I was not going to go with the crowd, I was going in another direction." For his father always forewarned him, "'Sam, never be someone that you are not. Don't try to be like anyone else. This guy may be a great singer, but don't say you can sing.' I knew who I was at an early age. I did not have an identity problem."

Although both parents were key influences in teaching and demonstrating Samuel's core values as well as molding and sculpting his personal character, his father, whom he revered, had the greater influence. "He was a man of character. I always idolized my daddy, and he became my role model. I always said that I wanted to grow up and be like my father. Not only do I look like him, but a lot of people say I carry myself like him, and that makes me proud." Even some of his siblings say that the apple did not fall far from the tree. His brothers and sisters laughed uproariously when Lubertha lightheartedly summed up Samuel in this way:

> Sam was a perfectionist. He was not going outside the boundaries of where he was supposed to be. . . . Anything he felt attached to, he had to try and do it right the first time. Even if he were challenged with a plain old game of stickball or football in the community, he was very careful how he picked his players. If they did not have the right ability, he did not want them on his team. . . . Sam had a passion for winning, and if he can't win, just forget it. So there was a girl that didn't play well, but somehow, she would end up on Sam's team. . . . And for some reason, the girl had an awful time trying to please Sam. In one particular game, they were playing and she struck out a time or two, and Sam was so mad with Wayne because he picked the wrong person for his team. He slammed the bat down on the ground: "I told you not to do it, I told you not to take her."

In the same way he strove for perfection, he was equally fervent in his faith. Whereas faith formed the foundation of Samuel's father's contents of character, the family's weekly rituals of church attendance and prayer gathering were its behavioral manifestations. Samuel said, "He was a God-fearing man and very faithful. During the week, we had family prayer, and all twelve of us would gather for about thirty minutes anywhere in the house—sofa, chair, or wherever you happen to be. My father's faith permeated into every aspect of my life" and, by extension, into his siblings' lives. Growing up, faith and family were two sides of the same coin. Like productive oxygen, both were interwoven into the formation of their very being.

If faith and family are two sides of the same coin, then moral character is its third side, the circular side that unites the two flat faces and gives them depth. For Pennie and Roscoe James, building noble character in their children was indispensable to their ethical development and decision making and to their moral compass and guidepost for living. They modeled character building through their ideals and actions, through their family talks, and through their nonverbal glances of extraordinary meaning. But when these methods failed, Pennie, the primary disciplinarian, did not spare the rod. Perhaps remembering the biblical admonition of Proverbs 13:24, "Whoever spares the rod hates their children, but the one who loves their children is careful to discipline them." Additionally, it was customary to spank during their era of growing up. Samuel speculated, "She spanked us basically because she was home and Dad was always working. She was a great disciplinarian. She was five feet five inches tall, but she carried a big stick." When the children would sometimes frown at their punishment, he remembered her saying, "We were going to appreciate it when we got older." But Samuel also recalled the softer side of the steely-willed disciplinarian who was equipped with a graceful readiness and vigor: "She was very sensitive, caring, and very giving. I am not afraid to say that although I am a guy, I got my mother's touch. A macho guy would not say anything like that." Notwithstanding his family of orientation's patriarchal bent, gender roles among siblings could be fluid. For example, the James boys had to wash dishes and clean the house. Hence, no marvel when Samuel says,

> I am domesticated. I clean the house, do the laundry, cook dinner every night, or at least every other night and all of that. A lot of guys do not do that. I learned a lot from my mother and what she did to raise us. My mom is a strong woman. And I learned from a strong woman. But I saw how she provided for us. We had three meals a day and leftovers for dinner. And that amazed me. As I got older, I saw how hard she worked. She would get up in the morning at six and go to garage sales to find clothes for us and other things for the house. I thank her, and every time I go home, I always thank her.

While instilling and building self-discipline in her children, Pennie not only taught patience, personal growth, self-empowerment, and perseverance, but at bottom, she imparted the importance of focusing on a long-term process and not a quick-fix solution.

For Samuel, who began working with his father at age ten, self-discipline and its corollaries were integral to Pennie and Roscoe's strong work ethos. "He started taking me to work with him to do smaller chores," Samuel mused. "But as I got older, he taught me plastering and how to install Sheetrock. I still have that skill and I appreciate it, too. I still do framework on homes." Although his daddy left school involuntarily in the seventh grade, "he was good with numbers and very smart in math. And it really amazed me how he would do his measurements in building homes," Samuel stated admiringly. "I looked up to him: he was wise on top of being smart at what he did." Unarguably, "building and tearing things apart" riveted Samuel's mechanically inclined imagination. "At an early age, I have seen my daddy take things apart. He would take down old homes and save the wood. I saw him take down mechanical things and that excited me as a fourth or fifth grader." At ten, as a hobby, he was building model cars and airplanes. Beyond his interest in fabricating model cars, he understood the value of repurposing and repairing household items rather than replacing them since the family had modest means. Hence, when Samuel was in the sixth grade and his mother's dryer broke, exercising his gift to solve problems nonlinearly, he traced its plug to inside the dryer, noting, "I could not fix it, yet that fascinated me."

Samuel's fascination with his frontline hobbies of fabricating model cars and airplanes, as well as his dogged determination and enthrallment in tracing the dryer's plug down all its byways, was instrumental in changing the trajectory of his life that day his seventh-grade teacher inquired about career paths her students wished to pursue. Clearly, Samuel was acutely aware, he said, of "what I liked, but I wondered what I would be doing?" Until his supportive seventh-grade teacher questioned her students about their career interests and arranged for each student to visit a guidance counselor, he had limited familiarity with career opportunities in his areas of interest. When Samuel met with his guidance counselor, he told her, "I like to put together model cars, airplanes, and other things, I like working with my hands, and I like math and science." She then broached him about technology, and he remembered his neighbor and friend, a band director, had also spoken with him about technology, asking, "'Have you considered technology?' I said, 'No, but I could consider it.'" Thinking that was a worthy idea, he told his guidance counselor that he would pursue technology, wherein she devised a curriculum replete with math and science courses, along with drafting. He stated, "It really prepared me for college." Caring teachers and guidance counselors who have high expectations of students can impact their educational aspirations and attainments.[1] For Samuel, this experience not only increased his college readiness, but it was also a random gleam of light that expanded his career boundaries. He remarked, "It opened something in me that I can control my own destiny by having the right foundation of courses and skills plus a high GPA."

But was it something more than Samuel simply having "the right foundation of courses and skills plus a high GPA" that would impact his destiny? William Jennings Bryan opined that "destiny is no matter of chance. It is a matter of choice." Then again, is it? Such a complex question, grounded in absolute determinism, poses too often a false dichotomy. Take this scenario for example. Samuel's parents held different standpoints on education that could have easily impacted the outcome of his life chances. Roscoe thought of education as a means of making a living, whereas Pennie viewed education as a means of living.[2] Samuel shared his insights on their diverse angle of vision: "As we got older, my dad wanted to take us out of school like his dad to help with his business, but my mom would not allow it, and she wanted us to continue getting our education. One thing my mother stressed was education. Even though her parents did not have money to send her to college, she wanted all her children to attend college. When my oldest sister attended college, it opened the door for everyone. She was successful and got good grades, so it was like a chain reaction. My other sisters wanted to go and be successful. We had the Pell grant that assisted us in getting through college." Coming of age after the civil rights movement, the siblings benefited from a myriad of federal educational programs to assist minority and low-income students.

A plethora of studies indicates that family bonding as a form of social capital increases school success.[3] Hence, the importance of Pennie and Roscoe James's influence in modeling moral values and developing noble character in their children served as a positive bridging experience for school and their academic success. Robert Putnam, in *Bowling Alone*, refers to two dimensions of social capital: bonding and bridging. The former refers to networks of homogeneous groups—that is, the family—while the latter is more heterogeneous—that is, the school and other external networks.[4]

Undeniably, Pennie was paramount in successfully bridging the gap between home and school; hence, her contributions to her children's achievements should not be undervalued. She was fully engaged in PTA and their academic and social activities. In stressing education, she was also their key supporter, telling her children to "be successful and get good grades and you will get a good job." Yet, Samuel acknowledged, "She did not know what job, but she wanted us to have a good job. It stuck with me." Teachers took notice of Pennie's high expectations for her children, their own expectations of themselves, and their self-discipline and prosocial behavior. Seemingly, Pennie's strict discipline, which they did not fully comprehend as children, paid off. "It did not take long for us to understand because when my mom went to school or attended PTA meetings, the teachers would say, 'Your kids are the best in class.' It would come from her disciplining us at home when necessary," Samuel surmised. Additionally, the sibling spillover effects of having older siblings who performed well academically factored into his success.[5] "We had the same teachers as my oldest siblings, and the teachers would always say that they know Lubertha, Debbie, and Mary, and they were very good students. It was incumbent upon us to be good students. We did not want to disappoint anyone. They expected us to be mannerly."

The prosocial school behaviors modeled by the older siblings helped to accumulate and build social capital for their younger sisters and brothers, along with the positive civic attitudes and behaviors of Samuel's parents in the community, church, and school, in particular, Pennie's participation in school functions. So it is not surprising that in Samuel's racially diverse high school in Elizabeth City, North Carolina, peers and teachers liked the James family and remembered their "good name" and their sacred duty to uphold high expectations academically, socially, and morally. For instance, Samuel recalled this happening: "I had a teacher who pulled me out of regular biology class and put me in an advanced biology class. I said, 'Okay, what you think is best for me, I will do.' He then contacted my mama and said, 'Sam is doing really well in this biology class, so we are going to move him up to advanced biology.' Although my mom pushed education, she did not know a lot about chemistry or physics, but she was supportive." Her parental involvement and encouragement helped to seal her children's success in the classroom.

Samuel's penchant for science and mathematics was equally matched by his love for art. He remembered, "I was heavily into art, and I loved to draw, so when I was in high school, I was thinking about doing commercial art and logos for businesses. But at the same time, I was taking my higher math and drafting—engineering drafting I and II." Who knew, at the time, that his predilections would pave a winning path toward success and eventually propel him to his present position at NASA Langley? Yet, it did happen in 1982 when his art teacher suggested a class field trip to NASA during eleventh grade. Samuel wondered, "Why is the art class going to NASA? We go there, and lo and behold, the technical side of me just really opened up and

I said, 'Man! I could see myself here. It would be awesome to do research, not knowing that I would ever work there.' I just did what I had to do in class."

Doing what he had to do in class paid off in the accumulation of human capital. Sociologist James Coleman noted that human capital grows out of social capital—that is, the collective skills, knowledge, or other intangible assets of individuals can translate into economic wealth for the individual and others.[6] So, after graduating from high school with honors, Samuel entered Elizabeth City State University in Elizabeth City, North Carolina. Having the excellent guidance of his seventh-grade counselor and having a strong academic foundation laid Samuel's success in his field of industrial technology. His classmates who had not taken the science, technology, engineering, and math courses, now referred to as STEM, were not prepared and had fallen behind. "They had not taken trigonometry and geometry. Even in my drafting I and II classes, students were not prepared, so professors used me to tutor them and to help them use T square on an architectural scale, the basic of drafting."

During his junior year of college, his professor and mentor informed Samuel that NASA was hiring and urged him to apply. "They probably won't hire me, but it won't hurt if I apply," Samuel mused. "So I went to downtown Norfolk at the Office of Personnel Management and the office kept me on file for over a year. The position I applied for had opened a month after I graduated from Elizabeth City State University. They called and said, 'Mr. James, we have a position for you at NASA in Aerospace Composite Modeling.' I could not believe it. I said, 'Thank you, Jesus. It was nothing but God.' The timing was so perfect. I always worried about what I would be doing. Will I get a good job or a career job to support me?" Samuel's stored-up social, human, and cultural assets finally translated into economic capital. He was "ready when NASA called," though he flirted with the idea of getting his master's degree in engineering at Iowa State University. Now Samuel can enthusiastically look back and say, "I do not regret it because good things have happened in my life since I have been at NASA. This job has been nothing but a blessing to me."

Samuel's dream job: The day Samuel was hired as an apprentice at NASA in 1987 was also perceived as a blessing. With a fount of knowledge in his field of industrial technology, the newly minted, clear-sighted, congenial, and compassionate college graduate saw the world as his oyster. His intellect and heart had found a home when he learned that he would work on building model airplanes. Surely, memories of his childhood hobby must have flooded his consciousness. To say the least, "I was mesmerized by the planes that I would be working on. I had the foundation, but I did not have the hands-on experience. Some of the hires had co-ops there, but I was hired as an apprentice straight out of college," Samuel quickly declared. He has flourished there and is well respected by his supervisor and colleagues. For most of his assigned projects, he has served as the lead technician, providing support to many of the agency's programs, including aviation safety, science, exploration, and aeronautics. He specializes in manufacturing technologies and serves as an engineering and/or project leader working directly with aerospace engineers and scientists in the design and development of complex projects and research components. For example, Samuel has served as lead technician on the following projects: to fabricate a storm radiation shield to protect the astronauts from harmful radiation, to fabricate and modify two-single L1011-Tristar's single-engine models to twin-engine model aircrafts, and to modify a 5-percent-scale 757 Boeing CTDIM.

In his fourth year of employment, his supervisor asked him to work on a new project, which incidentally two previous technicians had rejected. Samuel was assigned to fabricate a newly invented prototype loom or curved weaving apparatus, which was designed by a U.S. Army aerospace engineer. Its purpose, according to Samuel, was "to weave curved graphite frames to replace metal curvatures in the fuselage of planes." Unlike his previous colleagues who turned down the project, his father, Roscoe James, taught him to seize opportunities, noting "if an opportunity knocks, open the door. You have to fail first to be successful." Furthermore, Samuel welcomed a challenge and desired to prove to his supervisor that it could be done. With an anchoring air of vigor and vitality, he described what happened in 1991:

> Here is this young guy who loves a challenge, so I said, "Okay, show me what I have to do." The drawings I received were not formal but sketches by pencil. I spent one year on this loom. As the aerospace engineer was sketching these drawings, he would return them to me and I had them produced. He was amazed and wondered how I was going to do it. He had it in his mind how to do it but had no idea how to fabricate it. I was doing all of that. In fact, I came up with some of my own designing ideas that he liked. I became a co-inventor and ended up getting a co-patent. They had a company in Pennsylvania to build the automated one when this project was proven.

The aerospace engineer with whom he collaborated wrote an outstanding review of his accomplishment. Samuel received a promotion and salary increment. For some of his colleagues who were a decade or two older, the green-eyed monster reared its head at the youngest associate in the unit of fifty, who also happened to be one of two Blacks employed in the division. Overhearing some colleagues talk in the break room, Samuel responded, "I did nothing illegal. I earned this. They were jealous of this young technician coming in and getting a patent as co-inventor, so they were complaining that I was getting a quality increase because of my good work. The proof was in the pudding. You get this negative feedback from people, but I had positive mentors who promoted me."

An ebullient spirit, Samuel is aware of garden-variety jealousy and envy as well as deep-seated racism, but he does not focus his energy there. Although he senses "how people act and carry themselves," he adheres to his father's meme. "Life is simple if your heart is good. If I had an issue, and at times I did, I would go to my father with it. He would take his finger and touch my forehead and say, 'Count it all joy in the name of Jesus. You are going to be all right.' A few days later, my situation would be all right. He was so positive. You have to show God that you are working for Him and you have to have patience." Besides being mechanically inclined and being fond of a challenge, Samuel thinks patience and faith in a higher being and in oneself help to unlock the urge to reach one's full potential. Working on the prototype loom for the first year required a test of patience. He added, "I had faith that everything would work out, but on top of that, I love a challenge. I hate to hear people say I cannot do something. It is the spiritual part of me, the character in me, and the love of a challenge. We all grew up the same way. We have that same mindset. We can do anything at heart with Christ behind us."

With the mindset of having a can-do spirit, for a second time, Samuel's patience, faith, dedication, and hard work bore fruit when he was assigned as team leader to fabricate a model for an inflatable airlock project. This device would allow astronauts to walk from their habitat to the Lunar Rover, while on the moon or Mars, which is utilized for exploratory traverses. The inflatable airlock has many uses; an inflatable passageway is one of them. Hence, if astronauts wish to travel from their habitat to the Lunar Rover, instead of donning their cumbersome space suits, which were time consuming to put on, they can walk through the passageway without them. Samuel noted, "This is the first time we have done this type of work in my building. When it was time to fabricate the inflatable, my name was mentioned in a meeting as one of the technicians to accomplish the task. It was brought to my attention that Johnson Space Center was also exploring features of the inflatable. Johnson Space Center and NASA Langley were the lead centers exploring it. When they put Johnson's besides mine, they were uniquely similar; I was blown away. I worked in isolation, basically by myself, except that I did have a female technician who knew how to sew." Her assistance was needed to stitch the fabric together, while Samuel's task was "to fabricate what looked like a huge inner tube shaped like a scallop, which was ten-feet wide by seventeen-feet long." In the extensive process of constructing the model, he mentioned, "I had to fabricate three subscale models to see how it would pan out before I fabricated the full scale. The subscale was about four-feet long and three-feet wide." It is the responsibility of the researcher to design the product; however, it is incumbent upon Samuel to "come up with various techniques of how to fabricate it." He added, "Sometimes, I make my own tools, things I need to make my job easier." Samuel spent almost two years working on the inflatable airlock, and he received not only a group patent but glowing evaluations and a monetary award. In 2020, Samuel, one of the lead fabricators of the Non-axisymmetric Inflatable Pressure Structure (NAIPS) model that facilitates mass-efficient, packageable pressure vessels with sealable openings, was part of a group patent. Such portable structures are used on most spacecraft to provide compact launch packaging for structures that expand into larger functioning configurations once in space. This bendable airlock with sealing surfaces enables more efficient light storage and packing than what is possible with current inflexible designs. Moreover, it features a novel use of flexible, inflatable interlocking seals. Samuel is continuing his work with inflatable airlock technologies.

Being awarded two co-patents at NASA and being bestowed superior accomplishment awards clearly confirm Samuel's commitment to the agency's core values of safety, integrity, teamwork, and excellence.

In 1989, when Samuel's supervisor inquired if he would be interested in being the tour guide for their branch, initially he had some reservations about public speaking. Yet he did not allow an opportunity to slip away. "One thing I did not like was public speaking and had a fear of talking in front of people. But I did not take fifteen minutes or two minutes; I turned around and told my boss I am going to do it. I always told myself that I wanted to conquer the fear of public speaking." He mastered those fears. Since 1989, Samuel has spoken locally, regionally, nationally, and internationally to over one hundred thousand students in classrooms, at science venues, and at NASA, spreading his joy and passion in presentations with a program called ATOMS—Adventures in Technology with Options in Math and Science. "I have gotten numerous emails from students, and they say they see my passion and what I do, and they are interested in going into aerospace engineering or something like that because they see how much I love what I do. I say God is using me to capture these students." When he speaks with African American students who often have less exposure to STEM, Samuel feels that he is a more relatable role model. Clearly, Samuel is not only accumulating social, cultural, and human capital bestowed by the institutions of family, education, work, and the economy; he is passing it on to others. In return, he is reaping rich rewards. "It has been awesome from day one. Every day I go to work, I come with a smile on my face because I love what I do, and I wish other people could get a job and feel the same way I do. It has been an awesome job with NASA, and I have a good ten more years before I retire."

When retirement comes, Samuel may momentarily rest honorably on his laurels and perhaps find much pleasure in watching clouds float across the sky, while dancing under the stars or snorkeling in the briny deep. Yet one can surmise not for too long. For even outside of NASA, Samuel, the entrepreneur, inventor, and fabricator for other designers, continues to fabricate designs to solve problems. For instance, he developed a simple device to alleviate razor bumps. "My brother-in-law had an idea, so I developed it from a combination of frustration with razor bumps and inadequate products that did not work. We join millions of men that suffer from the inability to find and purchase the right products to fight razor bumps. I came up with a design, perfect for the contour of the face and head." A patent is pending for the T-Stone, which is designed to "dislodge ingrown hairs that cause razor bumps. . . . Razor bumps are caused when hair is cut with a razor and curls into the skin." Samuel conveyed that men who have curly hair strands are more likely to have this problem than others, and this includes approximately 80 percent of African American men. Other racial/ethnic groups also have this problem but to a lesser extent. After developing the prototype, Samuel found a company in Atlanta, Georgia, to develop the product, along with a complementary gel and moisturizer. The Army and Air Force Exchange Service is allowing Samuel and his partner and brother-in-law Derrick Wynn to visit military bases as a vendor. Additionally, Derrick did a casting on Shark Tank. Even though the T-Stone has received favorable reviews, Samuel recognizes that it takes time and patience to bring a product to the market. His T-Stone razor is now very much in demand. It is marketed internationally and is sold on Amazon.

Seemingly, his vast depths of knowledge and breadths of imagination are unquenchable. Samuel has assisted an African American pediatrician in Los Angeles, California, who invented a nasal suction and irrigation device with fabricating its prototype. This product is designed to irrigate and clean the nostrils. Although nasal suctions and irrigation apparatuses exist presently, none prior to Samuel's was fabricated as a unit. The owner of Wet Nose Technologies intends to market and mass produce this product.

Perhaps the rumination by Rumi, the Persian poet, "Let the beauty of what you love be what you do," sums up Samuel's essence about living. So while twilight sets on the talents of most, his seems endless. After joining a modeling agency, he became a commercial model for department stores and for print works. Additionally, he received requests for commercials and acting roles, such as reenactments for the *FBI Files*, the *New Detectives*, and the *Interpol Investigates*. Undoubtedly, Samuel draws key lessons from the Parable of the Talents in Matthew 25:14–30, where the master gave talents to three servants "each according to his ability." Equally embedded in the parable is the important tenet that we are all created in the image of God; hence, we have worth and gifts to give ourselves, families, and communities. Now, according to the story, after the three servants received a large sum of money from their master, two invested and doubled their returns, and the third one hollowed out a hole and hid his chances to apply his gifts. Like the two servants, Samuel, who is happily married to Valerie, and the father of Gabriel and Senya, has more than doubled his returns on the social capital given by his parents. It is safe to say that he has multiplied his assets to produce cultural and economic capital.

Hence, when asked about his most noble accomplishments, Samuel, a courtly mixture of courtesy and boldness, answered this way: "I am most proud of the person my parents have molded me into and who I am. I never had an ego, but I am proud that I am honest and people have trust in me. Even in the last few years, my own sisters have said, 'Sam, I wish I had a husband like you.' My own family was watching. I was humbled and it really made me feel good about that. You will be surprised who is watching you, and my own family was watching my moves."

Perhaps Samuel will be surprised to hear that while growing up, his brother Wayne was also watching him.

> Sam was more like my father. I could not ask for two better older brothers. Sam kept me grounded in high school. I had a little wild streak. Sam was very disciplined. I spent more time growing up with Sam than my other two brothers. Sam and I are so close. I have so much respect for him because he was so interested in being like my daddy. Little childish things I wanted to do, he did not do because "Daddy would not approve of it." I do not know how many times

I heard him say that. I said, "Can't you be a teenager for one day? Just be a teenager and loosen up." But Sam was straight and narrow. He was a tremendous light for me: the way he helped Daddy and worked in the church. He is an amazing guy. He got straight A's in high school. I was a year behind him and we had the same teachers, and they would say, "Sam did not do that or this." [Laugh] I had to follow in his footsteps.

His father would be so honored that his son is a role model for his sisters. Likewise, he would feel proud that Wayne followed in Samuel's footsteps; for indeed, he is bearing Roscoe James's good name.

Let us turn to the next chapter for a deeper understanding of why Samuel insisted that his success could not be understood apart from his siblings and his reason for softly prodding me to meet them.

## CHAPTER FOUR

# Quilting Threads of Congruent Consciousness
*The Good Name That Binds the Jameses*

Like a shimmer of golden sun breaking through the trees, their eyes spar-kled with delight upon the arrival home of Roscoe James Sr. in late evenings. His returns from a long day's work occurred shortly after the family finished dinner. Maybe Mary could be spotted near the top of her favorite pine tree awaiting her father's presence, or perhaps she, along with Pennie and Luber-tha, could be found in the sewing parlor darning and stitching outfits for the family. Other older siblings were likely at work in their dad's confection-ary store adjacent to their house. Younger ones were happily at playtime, taking walks through the neighborhood, or participating with friends in outdoor games like 1, 2, 3 Red Light, Simon Says, or Old Red Devil. How-ever, at the first sighting of their dad in his LTD Ford station wagon, they rushed home. Not only were they elated by his presence, but they also trea-sured the bounty of goodies he brought with him. And wherever they gath-ered in their home, he gleefully tossed a mélange of apples, oranges, animal crackers, assorted cookies, peppermint candies, ginger snaps, Hostess cakes, peanuts, and pecans for them to catch. In the summer, he brought watermelons and cantaloupes. With their dad's long hours away at work, Pennie aptly managed her brood of twelve's daily doings. Life, in its custom-ary streams of activities, flowed in a manner that was as routinized as the rising and setting of the sun and as rhythmic as the seasons.

During back-to-school season, Pennie would have her children lay out their school clothing the night prior to the morning bustle in the household. With only one bathroom, it was essential for everyone to be mindful of the next person in line for its use. Consequently, they swiftly managed their time so they could catch the three school buses that arrived, according to age groupings, to pick them up. Each of the four oldest, the four middle ones, and the four youngest took separate buses. After arriving home from school, Pennie insisted her children do their homework before break times with neighborhood friends, a leisure period for riding bikes, playing softball, picking blackberries, or catching insects and putting them in a jar. Dinnertime followed play. Although Pennie gave them a set time for dinner, frequently, the children became lost in play, so she had to call them. While

Pennie might have shown her children some leniency at play, according to Debbie, they were expected to adhere to three prescriptive familial norms: "We had to go to church, to go to school, and to obey them. All of us are regular churchgoers, and we still obey our mother."

These collective memories from childhood stir the siblings' sentiments, comforting them like a soothing and quieting touch softly laid upon their souls. Other stored-away memories stand out like Pennie and her oldest daughters preparing Sunday dinners on Saturdays to ready the family for their Sunday rituals. Her savory fried chicken, a favorite staple of their Saturdays' cooking fare, stood out as one of their traditions. Before leaving for an extensive church service, Pennie packed a basket of fried chicken wrapped in white bread. So succulent and divine was the chicken as it soaked through the bread that it acquired its own aromatic flavor, evoking vivid, mouthwatering memories of bygone days. Roscoe and Pennie would then pile into the station wagon, along with their twelve children, and head to the church that he built with the help of his brothers. The membership consisted mostly of immediate family and other relatives. Regular church attendance was their wellspring of life, a place where their spiritual selves were recharged. As a musical family, Pennie played the piano and directed the church choir, while Roscoe played his electric guitar. When the children were old enough, their musical talents, as Pennie liked to say, "made room for them." During religious services, whether it was their home church or a visiting church, the siblings were as certain as the movements of heavenly bodies that their loving, kindhearted, effusive father, with his triumphant voice, would testify. Each sibling has a different angle of vision regarding his testimonials, but the aim was strikingly similar. Roscoe's joyful utterances in the Apostolic Faith of the Church of Lord Jesus Christ were always about giving praise to the goodness of the Lord and what He had done. Here is Lubertha, the oldest sibling's descriptive lens:

> As long as I can remember, at least starting from junior high and when the rest of them were born, Daddy would take us to church. We wore out about three or four station wagons. If he could take us some place close by, we would all be in the station wagon with him. Our church headquarters was in Philadelphia, but Dad did not like to leave us home. So as we got older, he would take the older ones with him and as the younger ones got older, he would also take them. We would be in church conventions, where there were thousands of people at one time, and he would give his testimony. This was something we did not

care for, but he would do it anyway. He was not ashamed to give it anywhere he went. Many times, Dad would get up in front of thousands of people that we did not know and say, "All my children, stand up." I can visualize standing when my father would say, "Stand up, all my children!" They stood one by one. We would be scattered all over the church or wherever we were. We would almost get under the pew because we did not want to stand up like that, and he would wait for all of us to stand. If you did not stand, he was going to wait for you. People got used to it, so they would say, "Your daddy said to stand up!" And they knew exactly why Brother Roscoe was asking his family to stand up. You could not hide, so you might as well stand. . . . By the time the last one stood up, he was going to give thanks to God for all twelve children. We would say, "Dad, do not do that." We were ashamed because we did not want to be seen like that. But he would say, "You are my blessings; the Lord gave you to me. I am talking about my blessings." So we had to get use to that because he never stopped until we were able to talk for ourselves.

At times, worship can be a source of levity. Roscoe's youngest daughter, Terri, gave this amusing account of his testimony that brought a roar of laughter from siblings:

Growing up in church, my father would go to testify and he would always talk about joy. I sat with a group of friends, and they would slouch down in their chairs and say, "There goes your father to testify." He did not get permission. He would just go up there, and you did not know what he was going to say. But he would talk about joy. Who is this joy? Is this another family member? As a child, I had no clue what joy meant until I got older and was able to differentiate between happiness and joy. I know today the true meaning of joy and that is you have Jesus operating within you. When you have joy, you have help. Joy stays with you no matter what you are going through.

Roscoe's proclivity for full-bodied, whole-souled worship could sometimes provide fodder for a television sitcom. Wayne shared a humorous account of the night his father was so overwhelmed with joy he glided like an Olympic figure skater headlong into a set of drums.

Pennie purchased a new, shiny pair of shoes for Roscoe for Sunday service. She carefully forewarned him about the pitfalls of getting filled with too much soul with the smooth soles during service. Despite her warning, when he was overtaken by the joyful spirit as up-tempo gospel played, he ran, then slipped into a set of drums, perhaps setting off a little rhythm of his own. Needless to say, the ride home was a long, silent night, until a young Beverly innocently asked, "Are you okay, Daddy?" The family burst into laughter.

Roscoe not only had joy, but he possessed faith, vision, and imagination. Albert Einstein reminds us that "imagination is everything. It is the preview of life's coming attractions." For Roscoe, one coming attraction was his vision for building a second home for his family because the first one was crumbling from termite damage. Even in the face of doubters, he stepped forward on faith to give his testimony about the new home. Samuel commented, "He had bought the land but had not built the house that he erected without a blueprint. He talked about how happy he was about building a new home for his family, and he had a few church members giggling and laughing about it. One guy said, 'Where is the house? I don't see it.' He did not say the house was built, but he said that he was going to do it." Roscoe was unfazed by skeptics; his faith was sealed.

The James siblings' childhood memories of Roscoe's testimony about joy, faith, and vision took on a feeling of graceful readiness and a vigor of purpose, solidarity, and moral clarity. As adults, they are clearly aware that faith formed the firewall of their being and inspired their good name — "the immediate jewel of their souls," as Shakespeare wrote. The threads of consciousness, derived from such collective memories, bind their lives and frame their worldview, beliefs, values, norms, and core identity, as well as their sense of family and community. They have also left footprints of grace on their hearts and a strong sense of moral consciousness that have guided their core values. Faith in a higher power is the compass that guides the family; it is also the underpinning of other core values. More important, as Lubertha hinted earlier, Roscoe set forth as his family mission "to understand who God is and who His Son is as the ultimate reason for being." Thus, faith and family are conjoined values in the social landscape of their lives. They are like parts of a quilt: family is the quilt top, while faith is its backing. The filler or batting consists of the additional values, along with noble character, the binding that keeps the quilt together. In their own voices, the James siblings thread an oscillating family narrative as opposed to an ascending (rags to riches) or a descending (riches to rags) one. In the stories about their familial triumphs and failures, important life lessons like resilience and overcoming challenges are learned. Hence, such oscillating accounts are more likely to produce healthy families.[1] In the proceeding stories, a snapshot of faith and family is illuminated in various shades of light and designs, which, all being well, helps to produce patchwork patterns for piecing together their powerful family narrative.

Remarkably, with an age spread of twenty years between the oldest, Lubertha, and the youngest, Eric, as well as those siblings in between — Debbie, Mary, Roscoe Jr., Darlene, Karen, Shirley, Samuel, Wayne, Beverly, and Terri — they share similar attitudes, beliefs, and behaviors about faith and family and how the two shaped the developmental contours of their character. Unquestionably, their faith has served myriads of social and psychological functions for the family. It has provided a sense of community, social solidarity, social structure, and social control. It has also served as a guide for living, a way of meaning making, a way to reframe difficult life events, a source of solace and strength for life stressors, and a means of transcendence. Additionally, it has taught life lessons and helped to instill a sense of compassion, forgiveness, and gratitude. More important, the words and deeds of their father, Roscoe Sr., a paragon of faith and the chief moral arbiter of their Christian family teachings, devotedly fashioned the James siblings' spiritual and religious orientation and their sense of empathy, compassion, purpose, and service to others.

An old folk idiom reminds us, "As the tree is bent, so grows the tree." With strong roots, Lubertha, the oldest offspring, grew straight in her father's direction. She was the epitome of a positive role model for her siblings, playing a crucial role in nurturing younger ones, which had a spillover effect in increasing their social and human capital. Among ethnic-minority youth in both high- and low-risk settings, the literature highlights older siblings' role in promoting social and cognitive competence and positive development.[2] Here is what the oldest sibling had to say: "As the oldest, I did not have a sibling [to emulate], so I had to be a good example for all of them. My father would allow us to do certain things together. So if I messed up, that was going to be bad for them. After I finished high school, I became the second mother, rocking the babies and being the chaperon for them, as well as keeping them clean. That is what I remember in my life." She also watched the children on Sunday while Pennie directed the choir. Her memories engendered laughter, when she said, "Even in early years, I had to be the mom and keep the rest of them while she was playing the music. She had a stern eye. And if they were giving me a problem, they would not want her to see them because we would hear it the rest of the night." Lubertha shared this poignant story that illuminated her strong sense of family, her well-developed sense of empathy, and her profound sense of responsibility as a familial nurturer and caregiver. When she was twelve or thirteen years old, her mother went into labor at home. As Pennie groaned and writhed in intensive pain from an adjoining room, Lubertha became extremely distraught and she wanted to barge into the room to comfort and care for her mother who was experiencing labor complications. However, the old midwife forbade it and physically restrained her entrance. In her despair, she kicked her to loosen the tight grip, but she was no physical match for the midwife. Someone called her daddy, and eventually, her mother was whisked away to the hospital in an ambulance. She remembered the tears, fears, and furies of that scenario, which left its impact. Indisputably, even at that tender age, Lubertha bore the burden of a fully functioning adult.

Clearly, Lubertha did the lion's share of nurturing younger siblings, but Debbie, Mary, and Roscoe Jr. contributed, especially with Terri and Eric. Terri related the following two accounts. In her first amusing account, she described how her older, doting sisters came to name her:

> I will forever be [my mom's] baby girl, her doll baby, and her sugar foot, whatever she wants to call me. [Laughter] . . . On the other hand, I am my father's baby girl, but you know what? . . . I don't think I ever heard him call me by my first name. He always called me "Baby Girl." I think Daddy had so many children, I don't think he remembered my name. He never said Terri. I learned that my sisters Lubertha and Mary named me. One gave me my first name, the other one gave me my second name, and my daddy gave me my powerful last name. I guess my mother said that after having ten children before me, she probably just got tired of naming children, and she just gave the responsibility to my sisters. I said to myself, "Hey, I think the world of my sisters." I did not have a problem finding out later in life they named me.

In the second description, Terri illustrates the effects of older siblings on younger ones' social skills and perspective taking. For example, whenever Terri would have a misunderstanding as a young child about some familial dynamics, she indicated, "My siblings Roscoe and Debbie, the comedians in the family, had a way of nurturing the younger children and helping them to understand how not to take Mama and Daddy's fussing to heart. He always put comedy behind it, and my sister Debbie mocked Mama. And then we would go upstairs and put on a comedy show instead of crying about it. [Laughter]."

Since the literature is replete with studies supporting the important influence of older sibling on younger ones during childhood and adolescence, it is therefore fitting to begin quilting the thread of consciousness with Lubertha.[3] For indeed, she has heard more familial voices from the past and has experienced and seen what other siblings have not. Hence, having a longer lived memory and being a witness to the social dynamics of family life authenticate Lubertha as the siblings' griot, an individual who can pass on a repository of oral history and tradition.

## The Faith of Our Father

When Lubertha was coming of age, the griot remembered her father as a "jolly man who was devoted to his love of Jesus Christ" and his belief in Christ's goodness, a theme reiterated by Samuel. Family prayer was understood as a ritual for expressing religious devotion and for serving other functions. A study of 198 families who were religiously, ethnically, and geographically diverse concluded that family prayer served important functions and influenced familial relations in the following ways: creating time for family togetherness and interaction, building family support, and transmitting religious values. Family prayer also helped in dealing with issues and concerns of individuals and the family. It helped to create a sense of unity and bonding, and it helped to lessen family tensions during times of disunity.[4] For the James family, praying together has always served as a way to express their joys and sorrows. Here is what Lubertha recalled:

> My daddy was known to be a praying person. So we grew up building
> our faith in Jesus Christ. If any family would have health problems and
> accidents along the way in life, we always resorted to prayer. There
> were times we did not want to come into the house for family prayer.
> But whatever we were doing, homework or whatever, we had to put
> it down and come to family prayer. If somebody wanted to play a game
> down the street, you could not finish it because you had to get in the
> house for prayer time. We all gathered in the same room, usually
> the living room. If there were not enough chairs, we would pull chairs
> from the dining room, and we would get on our knees and pray at
> whatever time Daddy would allow. We had to get up and say a Bible
> verse or give a little testimony about whatever. Then my father would
> pray and remind us of who God is, and that is who you turn to when in
> trouble.

On numerous occasions, the family had to make that turn in times of misfortunes. Lubertha remembered such instances.

> Like any large family, we have experienced having the lights cut off or about to be cut off because Daddy did not have enough money to pay the bill to keep the lights on. But my father would always say, "Look, I am working and the Lord is going to make a way, or don't worry, the Lord is going to bless me." Somehow, if the lights were cut off in the early morning, before the light place closed, the bill was paid and they were on again. And you know what? I do not remember a time we were caught without having lights all night. If it happened, I do not recall. If the lights got cut off, my mom would find Daddy on the job, and he would say, "I am going up there by five." And many times, he would be there at the last few minutes, just before the utility company closed.

Since Roscoe had built up a surplus of social capital and goodwill in his community, his good deeds were remembered and rewarded. Lubertha alluded to such occurrences.

> There was a man who worked for the utility company, and here is what he would do if he had the red ticket to cut the lights off. He would say to me and some of my sisters who befriended him, "Roscoe James is a man of his words. You tell him to be down there early in the morning as soon as he can to pay it. I am not going to cut the lights off." He didn't. The Lord would bless my father with the money to go down and pay it. I never could understand how it could work like that until I got older and realized what faith means and what prayer means if you believe correctly. The Lord just blessed us, and I thank the Lord that we are able to be together and tell our stories.

Although Roscoe provided for the basic needs of his family, he was unable to meet most of their wants. Nonetheless, out of these childhood disappointments emerged essential life lessons of resilience, patience, delayed gratification, and even joy and humor that forged character and bonded the siblings. Stumbling blocks became stepping stones, as Lubertha iterated.

> If we saw something downtown or saw some of the other kids with this and that, Daddy would say that he cannot afford whatever it was, and then he would say, "You suffer the want of a thing." We were tired of hearing that we had to suffer all the time. If you cannot get it, you just have to suffer. But we learned to have patience and just wait. Eventually,

we got whatever we needed, but we did not get what we wanted all the time. So anyway, it wasn't a hardship. We did not always have what the other kids had, but many times, we did not know that we didn't have it because we had so much fun together in this family. We would make up our own games. In our large family, prayer was the first thing that guided us, and laughter was the second greatest joy we had together.

"Count it all joy, my brothers, when you meet trials of various kinds, for you know that the testing of your faith produces steadfastness. And let steadfastness have its full effect, that you may be perfect and complete, lacking in nothing" (James 1:2–4). This biblical precept of joy in suffering was part of their religious upbringing that shaped their worldview. As Samuel noted earlier, their father, Roscoe, counseled them to "count it all joy" whenever his offspring encountered adversities. Rev. Dr. Semaj Vanzant Sr., a theologian and pastor of Second Baptist Church of Asbury Park, New Jersey, offered insights into the meaning of this Scripture during a dialogue with Austin Bogues, a 2021 Nieman Fellow in Journalism at Harvard, and me on January 24, 2021. Vanzant said James, the brother of Jesus, wrote letters to early Christians living in Palestine giving socioeconomic commentaries and offering counseling on how they should live out the faith they professed. When these early Christians encountered adversities or trials, James counseled them to "count it all joy." Whether early or present-day Christians, the epistle of James urges individuals of faith to consider how to respond when faced with difficulties. People can choose to let "adversities destroy them" or they can allow trials and misfortunes to "develop them." The testing of faith develops perseverance and resilience, which leads to maturity and a sense of wholeness. Becoming all that God desires us to be results in a different outcome than individuals who choose to succumb to travails of life. "If you put your trust in God, everything will work out."

Roscoe Sr., as Vanzant suggested, put his trust in God. Indeed, he was the exemplar of joy as indicated by previous renderings, and according to Samuel,

He was so positive. I have never seen him down or never seen him cry, but there were things in my father's life that I knew were bad. He had a strong faith in God. Many times when he said everything was going to be all right, everything would turn out fine. When he talked, I listened. You have to show God that you are working for Him, and you need to have patience for God's time and not your time. When I tell people I have eleven sisters and brothers and they are all Christians, they say, "All of you are all still Christians! No one strayed away. . . ." We are imperfect beings, but we try to do God's will to the best of our ability. And it is through Christ that we try to do His will. We try to walk the walk and faith is in it. We are a close-knit family and we have that faith. And with God's help, you can do anything.

When Samuel voiced, "You can be successful with God in your life," their father was signaling to him and his siblings that embracing joy as well as faith is a means of overcoming difficulties. In essence, joy and faith are empowering processes rather than coping or depleting ones.

For Roscoe Sr., success meant serving others; even in random acts of kindness, he wanted to plant seeds of joy. Terri recalled he had numerous relatable sayings when making human connection to those in close proximity. "My father always had these sayings that could make people relate: 'I never met a stranger; Good morning, my sister; or Good morning, my brother.' He just needed to plant seeds. He was not concerned that the person returned his response because that was not in his control. He was worried about what he was supposed to do. He was obedient to [God] and the Lord told him to speak. Because he said that is all we are here to do is to give to other people." As previously indicated, resilience is integrally connected with success and joy. Hence, it was not surprising to hear Terri arrive at a similar conclusion as Lubertha and Samuel when she asserted, "I was able to understand that no matter what we went through, Daddy always talked about joy. I can always remember him saying that. Joy stuck with us so much that two of my brothers—Roscoe Jr. and Wayne—ended up getting license plates with 'Got Joy' and 'Got Joy 2' messages, respectively. Joy was so embedded in us that they wanted to have license plates [with that emblem,] and they wanted the whole world to know they got it. I have to say, listening to my siblings, we got joy."

Suffering is an implicit element of the existential human condition and of being a Christian. Consequently, whenever the James siblings encountered the slings and arrows of life, their faith served as an empowering mechanism and a way of meaning making. As Roscoe Jr. stated, "Our laughter and our joy healed all of our pain. [Whenever] the rain came, the sun would also come right away." The proverb about joy in suffering also helped to bond the James family. Lubertha mentioned, "My father would say, 'No cross, no crown.' He meant you have to go through something to get that crown. We all believe that in the end, we will all be together in our heavenly home, so it will be worth all the sufferings and headaches that we go through now. We were taught that. I am proud that the Lord has blessed us all to be together. We live in different places, but we are very close in our hearts."

Karen was close in the family's heart at the time she was diagnosed with a life-threatening illness. "I don't know where I would be without my family," she acknowledged. Besides family, faith and perseverance helped to sustain her.

> We all came from a heritage of faith. The reason why I say perseverance is because in 2008, I was diagnosed with breast cancer. When the doctor told me I had cancer on my left breast, I said, "Okay, what do we need to do?" Afterward, I went back to work. I shared it with one of my supervisors. And she said, "Why are you here?" I said, "What do you want me to do?" And she said, "Go home!" I said, "For what? That's not my battle. That is God's battle and I am still breathing. I don't hurt. I just have to go by the rules that the doctor gives me." The battle never stops. I saw how my father persevered through his Parkinson's. I see my mother who never stops and she is eighty-four or eighty-five, and I tip my hat off to her. Because I am a single mother who is raising a child, I get frustrated and don't know which way to turn. Sometimes I want to give up, but I think about her. If she can raise twelve, I can raise one. It takes a family or village to raise a child.

Although it is exceedingly beneficial for a village to raise a child, often the importance of older siblings' role as the caretaker of younger brothers and sisters in the family is overlooked.[5] Besides performing childcare duties in her family, Lubertha also chaperoned her siblings in activities permitted by their parents. Her role as caretaker tested her faith, particularly when Roscoe Jr., the firstborn son, stepped into his manliness and started to flex his muscles by rebelling against the family's norms. Lubertha spelled out this test of faith in attempting to bend young Roscoe's sapling to grow straight.

> I don't want to blackball him, but he worried us to death. I won't say to death; I will say to life. We did not die. [Laughter] But he did give us a challenge, but we always wanted him to do well. And we did not want him to cause Daddy and Mama any trouble. For some reason, he had to challenge us. If you told him not to do something, you might as well have told him to do it because he was going to try it anyway. So we could cover for him all we wanted, but somehow, he would always do

something crazy. We would say, "You know Daddy would not like that." But you know, he was still feeling his oats.

In terms of gender, birth order, spacing, and composition, the research indicates siblings' configuration can have both negative and positive effects in influencing the behavior of siblings. In general, older siblings are more influential role models. Additionally, having the same gender is more likely to enhance a role model's impact, especially when parent-driven dynamics exist such as gendered differential treatment and siblings' direct experience with one another.[6] Roscoe Jr., having the eponym of his father, adored his three eldest sisters, yet he yearned for a brother as a companion. In fact, he merrily recalled that when his first brother was born, he "guarded him like an armored truck." Since he had an abundance of feminine influencers, Lubertha could empathize with Roscoe.

> As I got older, I felt it must have been a little challenging for him, having so many girls around, telling him what to do and what not to do. We were doing it out of love. But for some reason, he had to give us a lot of headaches. We tried to love him as much as possible, and there was a time in his life when he began to be a little unruly in his mannerisms. He would not hurt a hair on anybody's head. But he did all the trouble to himself. He did things just to see how far he could go, but he knew his background. He knew that we were taught differently.

Although Roscoe Jr. rebelled against familial norms during his youthful indiscretions, he expressed deep appreciation and admiration for the role his older sisters played in uprighting the leaning tree.

> My sisters were so disciplined. I have some of the best sisters in the world. I am so proud of them. . . . Outside of my mom and daddy, they really raised me. And I am not just saying that. Even though they were women, they were more like male models to me because they played a role for me. They were my mentors and tutors. I went to them if I had to cry or have questions. They were someone that you could lean on. . . . My sisters were an amazing impact in my life. I tell them that all the time. During the toughest times in my life, my sisters stood by me. Sometimes people are with you in Miami Beach but not in Boston or Maine. They were my support system. Their prayers and faith helped to get me back on base, and they made me what I am today. I am not ashamed to say that, for I am proud of them.

Resoundingly, the sisters responded, "We knew he was special because everybody wanted a piece of him." As Lubertha endeavored to make meaning of his earlier defiant behavior, she offered this explanation of Roscoe Jr., who owned the first car among his siblings and who on occasions when operating his beloved Volkswagen, which was purchased by his parents, failed to comply with the rules of the road:

> I believe the Lord allows that to make us pray more. And we did pray a lot. And he kept us on our knees, and there were times he got into trouble, but my dad did not act like he was upset to the point where he wanted to cut him off. My dad would say, "The Lord got him; he is going to be all right." The Lord has taken care of that, and I can see why my father did not get so upset. He would say, "He [Roscoe Jr.] is going to hit a brick wall one day, and he is going to stop and see himself." And Mama would tell him, "Something is up the road for you, Junior." He just loved cars and would drive and not follow the regulations. You got to have a license to drive, and then he gets his license taken from him and he is going to still drive. We panicked! We are trying not to let Daddy know that he is driving without a license. That kept us on the edge all the time. But the Lord kept him and saved him. We are grateful. He can testify for himself.

And Roscoe Jr. did fervently testify:

> When Lubertha mentioned my mom's saying, "There is something up the road for you [Roscoe]." I realized what was up the road for me was Christ. I fell into His arms, and He has propelled me to where I am today. It takes a village to raise children, a family. My parents made sure we got it [faith] before we crossed the threshold, whether we allowed it to be useful in our lives or not. They were not going to be accountable for [the outcome since they had done] what God told them to do. Raise up a child, and they will not depart from it. I am honored to have my siblings to love me the way they did, and their love is what got me to where I am. Even though I ran them seriously crazy, it was only through the hands of the Lord, His mercy, grace, and prayer that it happened in time. All prayers have a resolution and all prayers have an answer.

The prayers of his faithful father, along with his mother, were answered for the reason that Lubertha evoked. "He [Roscoe Sr.] wanted his children to grow up being like him." And that way was to model their lives after Christ, to serve others, to be understanding and discerning, to be humble, and to treat others with dignity and respect. "All the values imparted to us from [our parents], I still have those values within me today," Debbie asserted. "My father was the primary person who taught me about Jesus. I have always admired his spiritual gift and his wanting to give to others and that has impacted me today. I know I have what I need, so the extra I have I can share it with others. We were taught to be an asset and to ask up rather than to ask down. [This is another way of saying not to be too impatient or brash.] For myself, in particular, when I began to play the piano, which I loved, my mother told me not to be pushy. My gift will always make room for me. So I have been playing the piano most of my life, and it is a passion I have." Mary concurred with Debbie regarding her parents' principles:

> I do recall my father, and my mother, always saying to treat people as you want to be treated. God loves us unconditionally, and God does not mistreat anyone. When we do mistreat someone, God will deal with us in His own way. Not only did my daddy say that, but he was a man who practiced what he preached. I would hang out with him, and I was a huge daddy's girl. I stayed a lot under Mom and a lot under Dad. I learned a lot from them both. Dad had a food truck, and when he came home in the evening, he would go to low-income areas and sell food. There have been times when people did not have the money, so he would give it to them anyway and say pay me some other time. He would always say, Magdalene [he called me by my middle name], "You never know what one is going through, and if I have it, it is theirs." That is one of the things that I remember, and I carry that with me today. And my mom was the same way. I am the same way. I am in touch with the needs of people. I treat people as I want to be treated.

Although Wayne, the ninthborn child, was interviewed separately in the initial interview with siblings, the first core parental value he uttered was "having respect for yourself and for other people. They were big on manners: 'Yes, sir' and 'No, sir,' and 'Yes, ma'am' and 'No, ma'am.' My father was very big on how we talked . . . and treated our sisters. He had the utmost respect for women."

Darlene, who acknowledged Mary's, Debbie's, and Wayne's memories that accorded with hers, summed up their father in this way: "My father was a good servant. I watched how he served others. When he would go into [housing] projects, sometimes they would not have any money and he would let them have goods anyway. It made me want to serve others." Within her church, Darlene devotes time assisting those in need.

> I will give two hours of my time every Saturday to help. I could be in the mall shopping, traveling, or doing anything. But I said Saturday, I will give my time and that is what I do. That is what I watched my father do. He also gave to the least of these and he also gave them a listening ear to their problems. And that is what I take with me today. I am always listening to what a person has to say, and I don't interrupt them. It is not that I have an answer to everything but just to allow them to express themselves. That's how my father, a very peaceful man, was. But what I got from him was that he was a servant to the least of these.

The generosity of Roscoe Sr., a servant to the least of these, was settled when Lubertha affirmed, "He gave more than others. He had a giving heart, and sometimes he gave more than he had. But that was just the way he was." She offered this example:

> Back when we were burning coal, I remember this particular incident of a family who lived very far down in the country, and what Daddy would do is order a ton of coal and tell the man to deliver half a ton to our house and the other half to the family in the country. It was about twelve or fourteen of them. And we would always wonder, why did he do that? The winter was not over. But he would always say, "God is going to give me more [coal], and I will help them [in the meantime]. . . ." I just remember he was always giving, and my mother was also very charitable. Anything she could do for somebody, she was always willing to do it.

Like Darlene, along with other siblings, Shirley, too, heard the importance of being a servant leader.

> Our parents taught us to be servant leaders. Right now, half of us are mentors to somebody. We are mentors to people because our parents poured that into us, and our aunts and uncles poured that into us, so we became what we were raised to be. We are mentors, role models, and we are popular people. We are well liked, but we are humble people because we came from humble beginnings. And we will never forget that. We are also not judgmental because our parents taught us about not judging. They taught us to give people a chance to be heard and helped.

Hearing the voice of each sibling awaken shards of memories for stitching together the family narrative. As Frederick Buechner voiced, in *A Room Called Remember: Uncollected Pieces*, perhaps we have a deeper requisite for doing so. "There is a deeper need yet, I think, . . . to enter that still room within us all where the past lives on as a part of the present, where the dead are alive again, where we are most alive ourselves to turnings and to where our journeys have brought us. The name of the room is Remember—the room where with patience, with charity, with quietness of heart, we remember consciously to remember the lives we have lived."[7]

No doubt Roscoe Jr. would agree with Buechner's sentiments when he interjected, "All of this comes back to you, hearing what Mary, Debbie, and everybody had to say."

> There were three Scriptures since I was a little boy that stayed on my radar, although I kicked and rebelled. But no matter how deep and how dark the clouds were in moments I was sinking, I would always pull back those Scriptures that my mom and dad always relayed to us. The first one was Apostle Paul: "I look not at myself: I look at the needs of others." I grew up working in my dad's business, even in the first, second, third, and fourth grade. I was with him and I have seen him wear that Scripture, which allowed it to become real to me, regarding what he did for others. Even when I was down in my folly, I would always go back to the Scripture and what those words would say. My father was trying to live that and he made sure his children got that. But one thing my mama instilled, and my daddy said as well, and I can take it back to what Debbie said, "Don't be pushy. Be who you are." And the Scripture that coincided with what my mom said was "Your gift will make room for you." Let it play out in time.

Reflecting on his journey from transgression to transcendence, Roscoe's third Scripture—"Fear God"—always guided him back to home port.

> I was the one, the rugger, when they said, I do. I said, I don't. . . . To this day, no matter what I have been through, the ups and downs, the hills and valleys, I can always go right back to what my parents instilled in us. My daddy would say, "People may not always read the Word, but they read you." My father and mom just didn't want to chastise us and to make us do the right thing; they did it. They were doers of the Word. It is easy to say the Word, but it is easier not to do the Word. Like I said, no matter how dark the clouds and the things

I brought on myself, I can always go back to that resolution our parents put into us. I go back to what my grandma used to say, "No matter what you go through in life, God is our provider, our refugee, and our fortress." I had to learn how not to worry and to have that be part of my life today. But no matter what I have been through, I can testify to all the love of my siblings, my mom, and my dad. They never turned their backs on me.

Perhaps Shirley's explanation of having a strong commitment to the family unit provides the most sanguine rationale for not turning their backs on Roscoe.

My mother and father taught us about love, faith, giving, forgiving, and compassion. It is amazing how we were a family of twelve who went without, but yet we had so much. We had a lot of love, faith, togetherness, and support that we embraced. It really filled the [material] deficit and the lack that we all felt we experienced and lived. Hearing my brothers and sisters speak, I now realize this. We were rich, but we did not realize how rich we were. We have a very rich story to share. And I would have to say that what I learned most from my father is having faith. We have all had our highs and lows. I attribute [overcoming] my lows to my faith. My family taught that, and it was intentional. It was an intentional lesson of survival, and of having blessings, breakthroughs, comebacks, perseverance, and of having triumphs over our lows. When we were having our highs, we were still humble people because hardships taught us to be humble. Hardships built our character.

Emotions of love, faith, and family gushed forth in Terri's talk. Referring to herself as the knee baby of the family, she lent further credence to the clan's solidarity: "I talk with my sibling quite often through calls, emails, and texts, but to have to sit here and to listen patiently to all of them talk about family—my family, I am sitting over here crying. It is a lot to follow, but whatever they have said, I cannot say that is not within me. What my mom and dad gave to them, they made sure everybody got it. All the way down to the baby. I say knee baby. I was the last girl of eight born [to my parents]."

The internalization of familial values was also evident with Beverly, who is the seventh daughter and tenth child of Pennie and Roscoe. Judging from Terri's interview conducted during June 2019 for this family venture, Beverly also "got it." That is, as a person with an intellectual disability, she internalized the family values of faith, family, love and togetherness, caring, kindness, humility, joy, humor, service, and empowerment. The former participant in the Special Olympics did not learn to speak until 1992, according to Lubertha. At that time, she would have been in her early twenties. One Sunday while attending a church service, the venue where she loves to sing and testify, the bishop of the church prayed for her. There, he spoke of her specialness and predicted that she would learn to speak. "The bishop said I was special and I would talk. I love bishop." (It is a story that Beverly delighted in repeating; for several times, she told it with glee.) Similarly, in her interview with Terri, Beverly voiced her deep love and appreciation for her mother, siblings, and her deceased father whom she alleged "cracked me up," meaning that he brought much happiness to her. During her talk with Terri, tears easily cascaded down her cheeks when speaking of his death. Likewise, she treasured the hugs and adorations from her mother and siblings, along with her desire to assist family members. For example, much satisfaction accrued from doing errands for Lubertha, such as picking up the newspaper or mail and assisting her mother with carrying and putting away groceries or washing dishes. In addition to helping with small tasks, she treasures the simple pleasures of life, such as going shopping, visiting her mother's sisters, greeting her friends at church, or having a breakfast of hominy grits and sausage. Much like her siblings, she is empathic. Memories of Michael Jackson and Whitney Houston, two of her favorite singers, still induce a tide of tears. Hence, one can only conclude from this summary of Beverly's interview that "everybody got it" is an apt conclusion regarding Terri's assertion about the family value system. In the ensuing story, it is equally applicable to Eric.

After listening to all his siblings attest to the importance of faith and family and how the two shaped their lives, Eric, the youngest sibling, spoke, offering his praise for faith and family as well as other values bestowed by his parents. "First, I want to thank my Lord and Savior for blessing me with such a wonderful family. I feel very fortunate as a young Black man to be selected to be in this family. My siblings talked about the Lord, life, falling down, and getting back up, and we are here to serve. If you have it to give, give it. It is amazing to hear my brothers and sisters talk like that. . . . I can say ditto to everything that has been said." The arc of their father's narrative shifted, given the twenty-year age difference between Lubertha and Eric; yet it shaped him in his father's image. When Lubertha was coming of age, Roscoe was physically robust and the primary breadwinner and decision maker; however, upon Eric's arrival into early adolescence, Roscoe's strong body was weakened by Parkinson's disease. Moreover, Pennie was playing a more overtly critical role in the familial decision-making process and as the bread-winner. The literature indicates that parental illness can have a major impact on the social dynamics of family life, particularly children and adolescents are put at risk. This is true if children take on a parental role. However, protective factors like strong social support and greater knowledge of the disease and positive coping strategies can buffer negative effects.[8] Eric's story is a test of faith as well as a life lesson well-earned and learned. He shared his story for the first time with his brothers and sisters during the initial interview because he wanted to reiterate what his siblings heard biblically.

> What changed my life was my father. They [siblings] have already said what he stood for, but one thing that touched me was when he got Parkinson's disease. When he became ill, all the brothers were out of the house except me. I remember one day getting off the school bus and my mom told me to start taking care of my dad. I said in my mind, "Why can't he do it himself?" I could only say it in my head because I dared not question my mother. . . . And that is when I noticed that he started getting sick and he could not do certain things. I became close to my dad when he got sick. And there were times when I got very frustrated. Here I am bathing my own father, shaving my own father, and clipping his toenails. I am getting him ready for church. I am doing all of this, and so why me? Can't he do it himself? I did not understand what it meant to be ill. I did not understand what Parkinson's disease meant. What I understood was that I could not go down the street and play. I had to go be with my father as soon as I got off the bus. My mother could not handle him, pull him out of the chair, or move him around. My patience wore very thin and I was fussing with myself inside. I had conflicts going on in my head about doing things that I should not have to do. I tell you, it was a conflict going on in my head. Why did I have to do this? I was learning things about how to do for a man. I was shaving my father, yet I had never shaved myself because I was not ready.

The experience of caring for his father transformed Eric and amplified his sense of empathy. Having been wrapped in a warm blanket of family love and faith probably helped Eric to adapt positive coping strategies for managing his father's illness. Perhaps it helped, too, that members of his sibling sub-system are predominantly female. A study of siblings' relationship as a predictor of empathy and humor styles in early adulthood confirmed that having warm relations definitely influence greater empathy and preferred humor style. The study also revealed "sisters demonstrated more closeness, warmth, emotional support and tended to have more knowledge about their siblings than brothers."[9] Traditionally, it is because women are more likely to adopt the caring, listening, and consoling role. As a young adolescent male, Eric was thrust into a reversal of family role as caregiver that created conflict for him. Yet, he was altered by it, which helped him to build resilience and develop empathy.

> It taught me how to take care of your own blood. That is when I became a man. When your parents get sick, we are there to take care of them. You don't know who is going to have to take care of you when you get ill. I try not to speak a bad word to somebody because you never know when God is going to use somebody to help you with your life. Our father taught me about becoming a man and taking care of your own. I said if this man can do it for me, then I have to do it for him. Growing up, my father taught me patience. As a thirteen-year-old kid, we don't know what patience is. We want stuff real fast and in a hurry. He slowed me down. I developed a deeper love for my father, and we got really close because he leaned on me. I had to be his rock at age thirteen. Though my love for him was challenged, I thank God that He kept those struggles in my head. I learned the mighty skill of having patience and taking care of [my father] who made it possible for me to be here.

While serving as a high school educator and student support specialist, Eric admitted that "I am like him. I give stuff . . . to the kids in school when they have physiological needs that can't be met. It is harder for them to perform when needs are unmet. But if God has given you something to give to a person, you have to release it. Be a joyful giver."

When Eric disclosed that he is like his father, "a joyful giver," it called forth an email reply of August 6, 2019, I received from Lubertha. Nineteen years after Roscoe's death, the email evoked thoughts of how his generous spirit still lingers and how it is also enshrined in the memories of those lives he touched. On the day that I received Lubertha's email reply, she had returned from the funeral of a close friend whom her father considered as his surrogate son. Notwithstanding his own twelve children he nurtured, seemingly, Roscoe always found a place in his heart for one more—a young man whose own father was absent from his life. Reflecting on his life, here is what Lubertha added: "He was a young man when my father adopted him and pointed him to Jesus Christ. He was considered as unlearned and without much close family, although he had many step-siblings. He followed my father around and Daddy gave him small jobs. Eventually, he was blessed to get a job with the city, working [as a sanitation worker]. [The job offered security, retirement, and health benefits.] The Lord truly covered his life and he was always grateful." Later, I learned the identity of Roscoe's adopted son, Leon Sessoms, who had grown up in Woodville, North Carolina, the birthplace of Roscoe, and was reared by his grandmother. According to Lubertha, as a young man, he worked as a member of an agricultural crew on a farm operated by Roscoe's brother and his wife for the county farmers. Lubertha recalled,

> When Leon became friends with our cousins, we got to know him when the crew workers would come to Dad's neighborhood grocery store. Leon was a fun guy who loved to dance, so naturally he drew my siblings' attention. He was known to be very courteous and loving. As field work slowed down, Dad would give Leon small jobs to do around our house and eventually he would take him on jobs with him. Dad was like a father to Leon and acted as his protector. Dad taught him lessons about survival and spiritual things. Leon could not read or write, so the driver's exam was administered orally. He had learned the mechanics of driving by operating various farm equipment prior to receiving his license. After Dad got sick and had to stop driving, Leon would happily take Dad on short drives around town and the nearby countryside. Leon earned a special place in our hearts.

Whether an individual was in a fair or foul social climate, the James household was a safe harbor for many individuals in their community seeking emotional, psychological, and physical comfort. Samuel disclosed this story of a battered wife who sought refuge at their home. After a neighbor's husband inflicted verbal and physical abuse on his wife, he chased her through the streets of the family-friendly neighborhood with a loaded weapon. She chose the James home as a place to shelter. She knocked on the back door; Pennie answered and invited her inside. The husband ran after her and demanded his wife come out of the house. Pennie stood in the doorway and blocked his entrance. Her five-feet five-inch stature stood tall. Her forceful, no-nonsense demeanor was unmistakable, as she boldly and affirmatively declared he could not enter. Snubbing his wolf ticket (empty boasting), the towering bully retreated in cowardice. Their respectable household was a sanctuary and, therefore, not to be violated, even at the behest of a bully.

Clearly, in the preceding vignettes, members of the James siblings stitched a layered quilt of joyful givers who are deeply embedded in faith and family. With each sibling jubilantly adding strips of matching and multicolored narrative pieces in various dimensions and shapes, they have helped to weave a patchwork of strong family ties and a binding of strong moral and ethical convictions. In spirit, they have produced a celebratory framework quilt, one that helps to strengthen the social fabric of family. They have also helped to build social quilts and bonding social capital. As the big-eye quilting hand needles, along with the little-eye hand needles, stitch through the layered fabric of social quilts and bonding social capital, reinforcing its strengths, it is also essential to acknowledge some shortcomings of bonding social capital, especially its impact on bridging social capital. Take religious social bonding, for example. Although it has produced a plethora of pluses, it has also created its share of problems. Alejandro Portes suggested the following dark sides of social bonding that can occur. First, it can impose excessive demands on group members. Second, it can exclude outsiders from the group. Third, it can foist the urge for conformity, resulting in limitations on individual liberties. Fourth, it can encourage downward leveling norms that reinforce and promote the status quo of the most vulnerable populations at the socioeconomic margins.[10]

Specifically, in examining the influence of religion and familism on secular civic participation, the literature indicates that religion can moderate the impact of familism, the primacy of family values over individual family members, and civic participation. In general, religious involvement is more likely to intensify the negative effect of familism on secular civic participation, especially if friendships and social networks are within religiously exclusive groups. Familism, per se, is seen as a factor that can reduce participation in secular civic organizations.[11] In effect, the insularity of social bonding groups can deny its members social networks and organizations that are social assets in building social capital, particularly if group boundaries as well as moral and behavioral prohibitions are rigidly enforced.

## CHAPTER FIVE

# Quilting Threads of Conflictive Consciousness
## *The Dilemmas of Duty and Living the Good Name*

A myriad of moral and behavioral restrictions existed within the James family's denomination of the Apostolic Faith of the Church of the Lord Jesus Christ. These proscriptive norms of the church were especially rigid while the older siblings were growing up but moderated somewhat for the younger subset of siblings after Pennie, who was raised a Baptist, and other members challenged the elders of the church. Wayne, the ninthborn, passionately illustrated some foibles of the church that enforced members' conformity to its rules and regulations, imposed gender constraints, and restricted educational opportunities, thereby leveling aspirations. Here is his poignant account and its impact on the family:

> It was devastating to my family and the dreams of my older brothers and sisters. My older brothers and sisters began to have apathy because they were told what they could not do. My middle sisters were told what they could not do so many times, they would say, "I won't do anything." One of my sisters lost a lot of drive in high school and she just said, "Forget it, I am going with the flow" because she knew she could not do something because of the church. It was against the doctrine and the Bible. Some of my brothers and sisters had the same aspirations I did, but because of the church, it went against their aspirations. It was man-made stuff and a man-made agenda.

When Wayne spoke of the prohibitions of "a man-made agenda" of the church, perhaps this is what Mary had in mind when she speculated about what might have happened to Samuel if he had been scouted by the NFL:

> When Sam was in college, if the NFL had looked at him to play football and if he had been accepted, my father probably would have thought playing football would have taken his attention away from his faith. He would have needed to get approval from the church, and the elders would have declined his playing football. I think that would have bothered Sam and my mother. We still speak about that today. It

[certainly would have been] a lost opportunity, but I look at it now as it was meant to be since Sam would not be where he is today.

Samuel's mother had permitted him to play football in college, but she did not want him to play in high school for fear of being injured. Nevertheless, he found a way. Samuel remembered, "In the tenth grade, Roscoe Jr. was sneaking me into practice, and Mom did not find out until two games before the season was over. I still cannot believe I did that."

Wayne and Samuel are merely a year or so apart, but Wayne claims, "By the time I came along, there was a change and I did not have any resistance to my dreams. I hold myself to a higher level because I did not have any resistance. Sometimes I asked the Lord, 'Why me?' Sometimes I feel sad I accomplished things they did not, and I don't feel worthy to have had accomplishments and a clear path to my dreams. But I still have siblings rally around me and support me, even in my aspirations of becoming a superintendent to change the mindset of parents and to effect social policies."

A college degree, considered an essential form of cultural capital in the United States and elsewhere, has become indispensable for entry to better paying jobs as well as an avenue of upward mobility. When most of the James siblings were coming of age, the church of their faith was in opposition to its members seeking higher education. Take Lubertha, for example. If Pennie had not convinced Roscoe their oldest daughter should attend college, the chances of other siblings doing so would have been practically nil. Hence, as the trailblazer, Lubertha bore the onus of having to prove herself by carving a path for her siblings' success. As she discussed being a role model, her gift of serene stasis, as well as her duty, was brought into play.

> When it was time to go to college, my father was not that keen or impressed too much about school. He said that we may get away from Jesus Christ if you go to school and be exposed. That is the way he thought. He was taught that. My mother played the most important part in persuading him to allow me to go to college, and of course, I was going locally to an HBCU [Historically Black College and University], Elizabeth City State University, in Elizabeth City. I knew that I had to do a good job and maintain my discipline as a young girl, and to do all the things I was taught to do that were right. If I had not, my father would not have allowed anyone else to go. The Lord blessed me to go to college, and I did not cause any trouble. It led me to be a respected person and to respect others. I did not have any conflicts going to school.

Without Pennie's intervention, this downward leveling norm of the family's religious faith would have undercut the siblings' accumulation of cultural and social capital. As Wayne continued to reflect on his religious upbringing, he offered this insightful analysis:

The more I learn about religion, the more it saddens me that the dreams of my siblings were abolished because of the lack of understanding about it. As far as education, the former elder over our diocese, whose headquarters is in Philadelphia, ordained others around the country to enforce policies. If [members] wanted to become teachers or march in the band, they had to consult with the elders. If you wanted to go to college or to seek an education, [the elders believed] you would become too worldly [and start] partying and drinking. College would influence you to become that way. That is why Lubertha is such a pioneer. Women could not wear pants. They were held back. You had to ask the church officials certain things, and it was always "no." But my mother convinced my father to give her one semester and to see what would happen. She kept her spirituality, wore no pants, and [wore] a hat all the time, and she did her church duties. She did not go wild and off the deep end. So she paved the way for others. If Lubertha had done otherwise, I don't think any of us would be educated. My father would have said, "I told you so." My mother received a lot of resistance from the church because she wanted to push her children to go to college. My mother was one of the individuals who blew the whistle on him [the elder] because he was taking money from the church, and that is why they did not care too much for my mother. She was a rebel. It was incredible how we had so much obedience to people who were taking money from the church and keeping us under subjugation. They felt too much education would expose them.

Wayne's perception of the church leadership, as well as its doctrines, has recently evolved. In his more idealistic youth, he was drawn to the charismatic preachers whose oratorical skills matched the likes of Martin Luther King Jr. or William J. Barber II. In such a highly emotive milieu of syncopated sounds of praise and worship, they appeared infallible. "It felt like the former bishop was perfect. I remember telling my mama as we came home from the Philadelphia headquarters, 'Bishop forgave our sins.' My mama looked at me like I was crazy. I knew the reaction she gave me was enough. I was thinking as a boy, the bishop was so powerful that he could forgive us of our sins. That is why I will never follow another man in my life. I will only follow Jesus Christ."

When asked how the restrictive aspect of religion affected him, Wayne responded, "I began to rebel a bit as of late." He continued espousing with a quiver of resistance running through him:

I am getting my understanding of religion. I heard a lot of Scriptures, but I did not know what they meant. But I am doing research into religion. I am beginning to understand the historical implications of the Scriptures. Where were all the educated people who could have risen up against the misunderstandings of the Word? They practiced modesty in dress in the past. If you wore pants, you were going to hell. If you wore lipstick, you were going to hell. The pastors used a few biblical passages to justify their actions.

We did not believe in celebrating Christmas and Easter. I had to explain not believing in Christmas [to my classmates]. I had this strange look. "How many people attended the church were affected by its doctrine?" [Perhaps reflecting on what he might have missed, he uttered this dilemma:] Don't cry over spilled milk. But sometimes you wished you had that milk because it was probably some good milk. But I still count it all joy, and all things work together for good. That is my motivation because I did not have to do all those antiquated things.

And one of those "antiquated things" was the church policy that prohibited women from participating in sports activities. Wayne remembered Pennie, whom he described as a strong woman, raising this issue of why her daughters could not play basketball: "My youngest sister played basketball and wore shorts. My other sisters could not do it. It infuriated my mother who had to go before the church." When Pennie challenged the status quo, Mary said,

We were proud of that as we got older. We followed right in her path as she challenged those doctrines. Dad became a little resistant at times. But with her intellect, I think he understood where she was going. It was hard for him to have insights into beliefs that he held for so many years. But Mom stood her ground with regard to her beliefs. Although we did not know why she challenged the beliefs at that time, we have grown in grace. Now we know that whether you wear pants or dresses, that is not part of your salvation. My mother stood her ground when we had to take PE [physical education] and could not wear pants. But we could wear culottes. She contested a few things with the officials of the church, but she did it along with my father. There were heated discussions about it. We look at where we are now, and Mom has been right. When the new bishop arrived, he indicated Mom was right. The previous bishop believed in rules; the one now preaches straight from the Bible.

Describing herself as "daddy's girl," Mary also conveyed more nuanced feelings and quandaries about gender role discrepancies in the family, noting, "Because of gender, Dad did not want us to get into sports. I thought sports were for boys. Yet, my mother had aspired to be a basketball player, and I found that to be a bit odd. It could have been because of our religion. My daddy thought his little girls should be in dresses." According to Mary, Pennie agreed with Roscoe. "I remember the femininity that our mother put into us. . . . I remember growing up being young ladies and knowing how to dress. Mom loved to see her girls in dresses . . . but as we got older, Dad taught us how to change a tire." This seemingly incongruous behavior suggests that Roscoe had a vested interest in teaching his daughters life skills for basic survival and self-reliance. Although Pennie and Roscoe relished seeing their daughters in dresses, she and other members challenged the church to change its dress code and discriminative gender policy. As the youngest sister, Terri benefited from the policy change. She had the choice to wear shorts, skorts, skirts, as well as dresses.

> My sisters were my Harriet Tubman. They grew up with a lot of can't, don't, and couldn't because my parents were very strict. Because of our religion, my father would say there were things we could not do. My sisters could not play sports or join the band because my father would not allow his girls to do it. That was when my father made all the decisions. It was when my father was still in his prime and had his strength. It was before Parkinson's took over his body. Some things my mother went along with, and other things she did not waver. But when it came to the girls wanting to do things in school, he won that battle in his prime. But when the tables turned, he could not make those decisions. He really could not put his foot down because he was so frail and fragile and the illness had taken over. My mother decided the rules and regulations by the time I was in high school. My mother said, "I got one more girl left." And now that she was in the driver's seat, she rallied around me to do things my sisters could not.

In high school, Samuel was eventually allowed to play football, and his brothers—Wayne and Eric—were permitted to march with the band. Yet their sisters could not. Like basketball, the James sisters, with the exception of Terri, were not permitted by the church or their father to march with the band. This scenario is somewhat paradoxical, especially since music fueled the soul of the James family. Both Pennie and Roscoe possessed instrumental and vocal talents, which they encouraged and transmitted their cultural capital, at an early age, to their children in the home and in the church. Although music served as an expressive outlet for the family, the development of the siblings' musical talents may well have assisted some in building cultural assets and promoting upward mobility. Myriads of studies support reliable evidence that students' extracurricular participation is associated with higher academic achievements, higher educational expectations, and other beneficial outcomes, such as improved interpersonal skills, reduced levels of delinquency, reduced dropout rates, and enhanced self-esteem.[1] For Pennie, academic achievement took precedence over extracurricular activities. Nonetheless, whether in the classroom or beyond, she expected her children to excel as well as become their best selves in whatever they undertook.

According to Lubertha, the first four siblings have musical talent, adding, "We skipped four until it came to Wayne and Sam. [Although he is now a professional musician, growing up] Wayne never showed an interest in music, but he is the director of band [at his high school] and he is good at it. My brother Roscoe taught himself to play music. When you hear him play, you would think that he was a professional jazz player. The talent for music skipped the rest of them. Anyway, even though some did not master music, they were always around it and have an inkling for it, whether vocal or instrumental." Debbie added, "Lubertha was a musician. I was a musician. Mary was a musician and she played the keyboard. And Darlene played the clarinet. All four of the boys were musicians, and three made it in the marching band. Sam played brass, but he took another direction. I would say seven of us were musicians." For Debbie, it was her dream to become a musician and march in the high school band. When denied this opportunity, she recalled her daily ritual at school of wistfully watching the marching band from her classroom window: "I would go into the classroom and look out the window and see the members marching and having fun with their instruments. Nobody knew I was in that room. I wished that I could be out there with them in uniforms. I thought there was no reason why I could not catch on to music in a formal way. But as I got older, I knew it was a new day. I could go online and learn my music and I can learn any kind of music I want, whether in pants or dress."

Laughter ensued among the siblings, as Darlene echoed Debbie's sentiments:

> I wanted to be in music while young, but we were not allowed to wear pants. I was in the band myself and my instrument was the clarinet. When I first started out, I did not have to be in the marching band until we had new leadership. And this particular leader made it mandatory that we all become a part of the marching band. I knew right away that I was going to drop out, even though I did not want to do so. I continued playing the clarinet for a while, but I did not feel it was the same as being a part of the rest of them, so I eventually stopped. I became interested in vocal music and enjoyed singing, along with my other siblings.

In Lubertha's customary supportive and cheerleading role as firstborn, here is what she had to say about Debbie's virtuosity: "Debbie does not step one step behind the band. And even though she did not get the training, God blessed her with a talent on the piano. She plays it hard and lovely. Others [would] rather hear her play than the rest." Wayne, too, paid tribute to Debbie's, as well as Roscoe's, exceptional musical gift, as he acknowledged Debbie's deferred dream while modulating his own ability: "I am not the most talented in music; it was my brother Roscoe and my sister Debbie. At that time, there were provisions by the church that said no way." Until his retirement in May 2019 as educator and director of the Northeastern High School band, Wayne's way of displaying homage to his siblings and to his protégés was being diligent and steadfast in his musical and educational pursuits.

> I came along at the right time, so I pushed myself harder because I did not have the type of resistance they had. I got my bachelor's degree and I got my master's degree in music education as well as another master's in school administration. After retirement, I would like to become an administrator in another state. Eventually, I want to get my doctorate in the next two or three years and hopefully become a superintendent within the next ten or fifteen years. I am pushing myself in these directions because I have a dream and passion to do some things—to help the decline in educational attainment of African American males. I feel I can make a greater difference as an administrator and as a superintendent than a classroom teacher in impacting policies for all children, particularly African American children.

Terri aptly summed up the restrictions of school, home, and church in this way: "We could not wear pants, makeup, or could not do this or that certain thing while growing up, but we still managed to stick together with all these can't, do's, don'ts, and wants to live a productive life."

## The Strength of Our Mother: In Praise of Pennie

"A family doesn't need to be perfect; it just needs to be united." Essentially, this anonymous quote is what Shirley remembered her mother conveying to her children: "My mom would say we did not need friends because we had each other, and that was true." Sticking together and being each other's best friend was also a clarion call for Samuel: "Our parents were selective of our friendships and associations. Father would say, 'Everybody is not going to be your friend. If you are in need, a friend may turn his back on you, regardless of how many times you help him.' When you grow up in life, you find out that you have a short list of friends." It is clear that sibling bonding was encouraged by their parents. When speaking with the brothers and sisters, one can sense the close connections between them. Their authentic, abiding love and affection for one another flow freely. The close ties are also a carryover from their positive parental bonding. In earlier vignettes, it is so evident how close the siblings were with their father and vice versa, but it is equally apparent with their mother. As Terri exclaimed, "My mother is an amazing woman. I just want to listen to her, and some days, I call just to listen to the sound of her voice. I will get her to sing me a song before I go to work. She will sing me a couple of verses. I am then ready for the world. . . . Just hearing my mother's voice is my cup of coffee. I get all fired up, although I don't need any enhancements like caffeine. I thank the Lord for another day just to see my mother. She is a powerful woman. She is eighty-four years of age and still says, 'I got it.' Mom, I know you 'got it,' but can I do something for you today? Can you just go somewhere and sit down? You are off duty. Can I rub your feet or clip your fingernails or toenails?" Terri offered those effusive praises for Pennie, and additional ones poured forth:

> She is the strongest woman I know. She was the biggest fan in my life when it came to my high school and collegiate sporting life. She came to all my basketball games and my volleyball games in high school and in college. She was the first one through that door of the gym, as she walked pigeon-toed with her purse in her left arm, heading to the same seat in the gym. No one sat in her seat because they knew Pennie James

was coming. She was a person who lived vicariously through me, and she liked basketball, so I took on basketball. I tried to be like Daddy and take piano lessons, and I said, "This is not for me." My mother was trying to get me to play the piano, and I said, "No, I need to be moving." So my mother allowed me to try out for basketball. And my mother got me to the games and made sure to say, "If you are going to play, you make sure you study your books now. If you fail, you're going to have to quit." I knew I wanted both worlds—to be a good student and to be a student athlete. I knew I had to study my books, and I knew I had to play sports. I balanced both of them with the help of my mother and my siblings. Father was not going to come because he did not want me to play anyway. My mother, brothers, and sisters, who could, came to support me. I was able to make it through high school being an athlete without having to quit the team, and I made it to college with an academic scholarship. I did not have to play basketball because I had an academic scholarship. But my mother still put her foot down, even when I was in college. She meant what she said. Don't try to second-guess her! [This expression is used when anticipating someone's action.]

Wayne learned quickly not to second-guess Pennie when he attempted to fit in with his peers who took general-level courses. "Few African American guys were taking upper-level courses, so Pennie James was not going to allow her children to take general-level courses when they could do better. She was a pioneer and went against the grain. She did not take any mess. You could not pull anything over her eyes. She would say, 'You can't show me a red apple.'" Laughing, he admitted that he did not know its meaning literally, but metaphorically, he intuitively understood the phrase to mean do not attempt to deceive her. Both Shirley and Darlene, respectively, also affirmed Terri and Wayne's view that the siblings did not second-guess Pennie, who was described as a strong, independent disciplinarian by her offspring. Shirley declared, "My mother was a disciplinarian. She was always the one that lined up the punishment if we were bad and got out of line. She is very independent and the strongest woman I know. She is a no-nonsense kind of woman, but her strength is manifested in all of us, especially the girls and now the women that we have become." Echoing similar sentiments, Darlene affirmed Shirley's viewpoint: "My mom is a very independent woman. She always told us to get out there and do things for yourself. Do not depend on anybody. Not that you do not need any help, but just try to find out how you can do things for yourself. In her eighties, she still is.

Having arthritis has slowed my mother down a lot. But if I say that I will take groceries from the car, or if any of us try to do things to help, she will say, 'no.' Her independence has impacted me. It is not that I don't need anyone, because we all do. Rather, it has just made me more independent. The more independent I am, the more I discover who I am as a person."

In addition to the strong support Pennie provided, she imparted lessons that reinforced discipline, self-confidence, respect, and a sense of empowerment. Terri remarked, "My mother raised me to be patient, to treat people right, and to be punctual. Punctuality was my mother's big pet peeve, and my sisters and brothers could attest to that. You would rather wait on someone before they wait on you. Be wherever you have to be on time. Do it right, be your best, and do your best. If you don't have on your best, go buy your best, and treat people right."

Jim Henson, the cartoonist and puppeteer who created the Muppets, offered this kernel of insight: "Kids don't remember what you try to teach them. They remember what you are." Quite the contrary, the siblings not only remember what Pennie taught them; they remember her especially as the engineer of upward mobility. Shirley exhorted, "She is the one that drove us to get an education." Similarly, Wayne, along with other siblings, contended their mother propelled them toward higher education.

> Mother believed in education. She wanted to go beyond her high school diploma. She got married at nineteen, and she committed herself to raising children, but she wanted to go further. It was my understanding that she wanted to be a schoolteacher. She pushed education because she knew it was something no one could take from you. Education would empower you. It would give you an opportunity to make a better living than she had. I was the first one to go away to college. I went to East Carolina University for music education. I wanted to become a band director, but at the time, Elizabeth City State University did not have music education as a major. I had other brothers and sisters who wanted to major in music, but they could not because it was unavailable. Except for Eric, my other brothers and sisters went to Elizabeth City State University, and a few attended the College of Albemarle. I knew going away would be a tremendous burden on my parents, so I talked to my mom about it. And she talked to my father, and they made it happen. I thought I would have to go to Elizabeth City State University because my father needed me there to help him. But the day they told me that I could go to East Carolina

University, I cried like a baby. I made it happen. I worked two or three jobs to keep myself in school. It took me a little longer, but I did not give up. I felt pressured not to blow this opportunity and that kept me motivated. My mother was really big on "if that is what you want to do, we are going to provide the resources for you." And they did.

Social scientists investigating cognitive skills and attitudinal behavioral traits have long noted their prominence in influencing life chances and outcomes of individuals and groups. Although both are important, a body of evidence supports that noncognitive traits and behaviors are more vital than cognitive skills. Examples of attitudinal and behavioral traits include locus of control—the belief regarding whether one's self or external factors control one's destiny, educational aspirations and expectations, and self-esteem.[2] Judging by the outpouring of praises piled on Pennie, not only did she possess a strong sense of the aforementioned noncognitive characteristics and skills, but she also transmitted them to her children. Additionally, Pennie possessed relatively high cognitive skills. Granted she did not have the opportunity to attend college, it was still an aspiration for herself and for her children. It was also likely that during Pennie's coming of age in the late 1930s, 1940s, and early 1950s, her educational attainment was higher than her peers in the surrounding community. A plethora of studies supports that a family's socioeconomic status—measured by education, occupation, and income—is also related to children's academic outcomes. In general, previous studies have examined the household unit or the income of the father. But now, several scholars are examining how maternal education level is related to children's academic functioning, which includes cognitive skills, academic achievement, and educational attainment.[3] As such, these heretofore unrecognized maternal assets may be parlayed into social and cultural capital for their children. In a tone of effortless admiration, Wayne conveyed the maternal capital of Pennie and its outcomes in this vignette: "She took me to my first concert, and all the other concerts, and supported me in what I wanted to be and do. When I became band director in 1991, she went to all my concerts. She was very proud of the fact that I attended college and was able to make a success of it. She was very concerned about my getting wrapped up in some other parts of college life. I kept her concern in mind since I was the first to leave home and I did not want to have any resistance, mainly from my father."

Purportedly Pennie had aspired to be an educator, so she championed higher learning for her children and advocated for freedom of choice in their career aspirations and extracurricular activities, in particular her younger children. Hence, she was proud to see her offspring's educational attainments. Additionally, she was honored to see Wayne, Terri, and Eric become educators in the public school system, a dream deferred for her, yet actualized through three of her youngest children. In observing students under their tutelage, Wayne, Terri, and Eric look back with nostalgic longing for the values that Pennie and Roscoe instilled in them and wish those same values could also be imparted to their students and to their students' parents. Although they are clearly cognizant of structural inequities impacting their students' educational aspirations and attainments, they are also mindful that empowering attitudes, values, and behaviors matter for upward mobility. Wayne lamented what he observed as the lack of expectations for students and the breakdown in accountability, authority, civility, and respect in the school, family, and community. In his view,

As opposed to my parents of forty years ago, having personal drive is like day and night. My parents were pushing for education to better themselves. Some parents just want their kids to go to school to eat or to have some free time for themselves. It is becoming more apparent today. It saddens me because I deal with it in my school, and I see the change in parents' attitudes over the twenty-seven years since I have been at that school. One change is accountability. My parents only wanted to see A's and B's. My parents would have had a conference with teachers if we made a C grade. If you were putting forth effort that would be a different story. I brought a couple of C's home, and the teacher said that I had some issues with taking honors courses because I wanted to be with my friends who were African Americans. Their parents were not pushing them to take tougher courses. My mother pushed me to do that. I was not taking classes with my friends; I was taking classes with people who did not look quite like me, and I was uncomfortable. I don't see that same push today from parents. I see students today who should be in those AP classes, but they do not push themselves to do that, nor do they have parents to push them in that direction. Without that push, they have more of a challenge in school. Often, I tell the children about the Little Rock Nine, because during the 1950s, their parents wanted them to have a better education. This day in time, the children do not have that push, and they are not intimidated if they go home with an F because the parents do not worry too much.

My mother attended most of the conferences: she was consistent. She met the teacher away from the children, and the teacher was always right. Today, it is "not my child; you have the wrong child." I have had experience with that a few times myself. They take the side of the child more than the teacher, including the principal. I think parents are crippling them and not encouraging them to be all they can be. This is in opposition to what I was taught. I was taught to listen to the teacher if she says, "Stop talking!" If she says when to go to the restroom, that is when you go. There were no ifs, ands, or buts about it; you were to respect authority. And for the most part, it is a different concept now.

While Wayne is encouraging, motivating, and preparing his students to develop their cognitive and noncognitive skills, his goal, as mentioned previously, is to have a larger impact in effecting school policies and in reaching a broader community to educate and motivate families. For it is Wayne's belief, and also what he tells his students, "if you educate the brain, it is more powerful than any bullet. If you begin to think for yourself, you begin to become empowered. I think this country is more afraid than anything else of [when] people who were once regarded as inferior become empowered with education."

When Terri, a dedicated special education teacher, thinks about the low educational expectations, the lack of discipline, and incivility as she walks the halls of her school, she sometimes utters silently,

Mom and Dad, I wish you could walk these halls and give these children what you gave us. They would at least have a 50 percent chance of survival. The discipline is missing today. Some parents may have it, but the true put-your-foot down is missing. And I thank the Lord for my parents and all the things we could not do. They explained the things we could not do. The spankings that we received molded us. Every time I turned around, she was spanking me and that molded me. My parents should see what the kids are like today. I can say my parents really put their hands on me, showing me how to love and how to put the Lord first in everything I do.

Then Terri added, "Siblings, I love you all and I talk about you all the time." All the siblings spontaneously responded in unison, "I love you, too."

The unprompted display of love and affection between the siblings overwhelmed Eric, a middle school educator, who enjoys teaching. Agreeing with Terri, his glowing parental tribute was suddenly interrupted by a staccato cry: "I cannot repay my wonderful father and mom for what they did." After being comforted by his siblings' reassuring words, "It's all right baby" and "Amen!" Eric continued to speak: "My executive director on my job who makes ten times as much as I do, asked me, 'Why are you always so happy?' That was ten years ago and I will never forget. Why shouldn't I be happy? Here is why I am so happy [referring to his siblings during a telephone conference call]. My joy is overflowing all the time. These kids nowadays don't have what we have. They are so messed up and lost in the world. I could have been born out on the streets. I could have been born with no dad or whatever. God put me in this place, I did not even have a choice of where I was born." Although Eric had no choice in the selection of his biological parents, he had a hand in giving back what he "got" from them and his siblings. And what he acquired from his parents were those value-added ingredients that have become the staple of his life mission to pass on to others. Samuel quickly interjected this impromptu story to support his brother's calling, while Eric gathered his composure. He recalled that one student whom Eric had once coached and mentored, while serving as an assistant football coach at his school, was scouted for football with the offer of a scholarship by the University of Delaware. His parents could not take him there because they were separated and living in different states. "Eric stepped in and used his own money and gas to take him to the game at the University of Delaware. They thought Eric was his father and he played it off. When Eric told me this story, it was touching that he was there for the young man." Eric continues to be there for so many others like that football player.

## The Work Ethic

Accountability, adaptability, discipline, dedication, dependability, durability, motivation, civility, optimism, honesty, and efficiency are character traits Pennie and Roscoe instilled in their offspring. They also fostered a strong work ethic. However, Wayne, Terri, and Eric observed that these enduring qualities they embody are waning in their educational milieu. Their anecdotal observations are buttressed by scholars who examine such subjects as the decline in civility,[4] along with generational differences in work ethic.[5] Success, whether in school or in the workplace, is interconnected with these attributes. The maxim, "The dictionary is the only place where success comes before work," attributable to Vince Lombardi, has elements of truth. It is what Wayne, along with his siblings, learned from Pennie: "My mother would say there are no shortcuts to success; you have to work for it." Judging by Eric's rather hilarious account of assisting Pennie at her Saturday auction hunts for antiques, he, too, quickly learned the lesson that "God gives every bird its food, but He does not throw it into its nest," declared J. G. Holland.

Describing his mother, a woman with a powerful voice, as "stronger than ten men," he iterated what it was like to watch Pennie work as he tagged along with her on Saturdays:

This woman knew she had a purpose. On Saturday morning, we ran an antique shop. We had to get up at 5:30 A.M. and go to garage sales. What kid wanted to get up at 5:30 A.M. in the morning on Saturday? [Laughter] Thinking silently, I said, "Can I sleep or watch cartoons?" I am ready to chill out. But oh no! She is calling us at 5:30 A.M. or 5:45 A.M. I am trying to get some diva sleep and relax. [Laughter] Yet she came up the stairs yelling my name. I said to myself, "There are five hundred other people in this house, so why do I have to work on Saturday?" I had to get ready to punch a clock. My mother would scope out these garage sales and circle them and then go to different streets. I would say, "Mom, do not get in line with the mailman: we are going to everybody's house." My mother had a method to the madness. She had to feed our family, so she did whatever it took. She knew the reason was bigger than her. If she did not do the job, we were going to starve. Now I understand her reasons. She taught me how to hustle and to make ends meet. She was always talking about making ends meet. I always hoped my ends would get really close. We were trying to make it. Everything must go, half off, and half off of that half. And if you brought your P [purchasing] card, you could get a discount. She would look at a certain chair for a hundred dollars, and she was going to take the price down to fifty. She would tell the story, "I got twelve children at home. I want to know if you would take fifty dollars for this chair," knowing that she was going to get three hundred dollars for it. [Laughter] She was so magical. She would take one hundred dollars and go buy one hundred dollars' worth of stuff and put it in her auction and then go flip the money. We packed up that long station wagon and that thing would be packed from the bumper to the back. [Laughter] If we didn't have any more room for a shelf, we would come back and get it. I would shine up the furniture. I did not understand [the significance of what she was doing] until I saw her take the money she made to feed the family. I watched my mom's work ethic. Her work ethic was ten times that of a regular person. And now I understand why she did it—because she had to take care of all these people. We wanted stuff, but we got what we needed. There was no savings account. She had to account for every penny.

This lesson vis-à-vis managing money is exactly what Wayne also remembered about his father, an industrious worker, who instilled in him, "You spend on needs first and then on your wants." It was imperative not to waste time or money on frivolous pursuits. Roscoe Jr., Samuel, and Wayne, who all worked tirelessly with their father in his plastering and drywall business, can attest to that belief. They noted his meticulous work ethic and the long hours of providing the best quality customer care. In fact, at times, they had difficulty sustaining his work pace and endurance. Wayne shared how his father's work ethic and entrepreneurial acumen influenced him:

> We worked with my dad mostly on Saturdays, during school breaks, and during summers. In that way, he could keep an eye on us and teach us how to run the business. I use some of those examples today in my business. I am a jazz musician and I play at several restaurants. I am one of those who go around and play for different functions. My business is called Wayne P. James Entertainment. I have also been a full-time director at my high school for twenty-seven years. So I took some of the same values from him. He was on time, kept his word with people, and he did quality work. He was very pleasant with the customers. That is what I always saw while growing up. When my father would do an estimate for a job on a person's house, he was very polite and mannerly, and he would always say, "Yes, ma'am" and "No, ma'am." For someone who owned his business and who never took any business courses, he was my biggest influence in terms of the key aspects of having a successful business. Since he stressed the importance of being on time, being fair with people, being honest, and doing quality work, I picked up those qualities from him. And my business has also become successful.

Shirley aptly summed up the prominence of the work ethic in all the siblings' upbringing: "My mother and father taught us to have the amazing work ethic that we have today. Both of my parents were entrepreneurs and taught us about survival. I don't know if I would have ever understood hard work if they were not entrepreneurs. And I saw them work. If they did not work, we did not eat. And we were never on public assistance, which is extraordinary. It is extraordinary today, let alone back in those days not to have to raise a large family on public assistance. It was not our experience." Mary would concur with Shirley that welfare was definitely not their experience because Pennie had instilled in her children the importance of being self-sufficient. Moreover, she never wanted her children to label themselves as poor despite having limited monetary resources. At times, while growing up in a household of twelve children, Wayne felt that having welfare assistance would ease the burden on his parents, so he hinted a few times to his father about some benefits of receiving welfare.

> My father would say, "No way!" When I would tell our father, do you know how much money you can get with twelve children? He did not like that, and he went into a rant. He would say, "Not in this household; your butt will get out and work." He saw it as cyclical. We had to go through the projects while riding the school bus, and at twelve o'clock P.M. you would see these fathers sitting on the porch with nice cars. My father was never home that time of day. These people knew their way around the system. I hinted that to my father, and he reprimanded me. He worked so hard, and I was concerned about him. He said, "Son, don't you bring that kind of thinking in this house!" I would cry sometimes because he was working so hard. I was trying to tell him how to beat the system. Instead, I got the work ethic from him.

Roscoe Sr.'s strong work ethic was undoubtedly influenced by the religious undertones of his upbringing. Numerous biblical passages refer to the importance of work—for example, Proverbs 13:4, which states, "The soul of the sluggard craves and gets nothing, while the soul of the diligent is richly supplied." More specifically, the Protestant work ethic, an idea introduced by sociologist Max Weber, is a pertinent cog of the American value system.[6] Underlying the Protestant work ethic are four basic tenets: (a) "Working hard is honorable and is a calling by God," (b) "Economic success is a sign of God's grace," (c) "An individual is responsible for controlling one's action and living a moral life," and (d) "An individual should abstain from wasteful materialism that results from one's hard labor."[7] Of course, the Protestant work ethic is irrespective of religious inclination and can be found across Western and Eastern cultures. In fact, some evidence indicates it may be stronger in certain Eastern cultures.[8]

Whether the James siblings' strong work ethic is derived from the aforementioned four tenets is not the specific focus of discussion. Rather, the interest here is to garner anecdotal insights into the linkage between the James siblings' strong work ethic and their perceptions of ethnic and class identity. If a connection exists, then how do these factors affect their attitudes toward welfare, especially in the context of their care ethics "for the least of these"? Wayne's comments, regarding his father's feeling about welfare, stirred my imagination in this direction, especially since the Protestant work ethic emphasizes individual responsibility and deemphasizes structural and cultural constraints. Moreover, my curiosity was also piqued when Wayne indicated that he identified more with middle-class whites. It is clear that he has his father's work ethic, but to some degree, he adheres to his father's perspective of welfare when he articulates, "There are some people I know that need the welfare system, but it is also a way of keeping you in your place. If you know that you have a check coming [monthly] and [you] just sit on the porch all the time, with no job, [some] people are satisfied with doing that." To gain insights into the siblings' class and ethnic identity, I asked them the following question: In terms of your values, beliefs, and attitudes, do you feel closer to (a) poor or working-class Blacks, (b) middle-class Blacks, or (c) middle-class whites? Of the ten who responded, one felt closer to middle-class whites, three felt closer to middle-class Blacks, and three felt closer to poor or working-class Blacks, and three had more fluid feelings, meaning they identified with more than one category. Findings of the seminal study "Ethnic Differences in Endorsement of Protestant Work Ethic: The Role of Ethnic Identity and Perceptions of Social Class" uncovered that when comparing ethnic identity, Blacks were higher than whites, but they also had a lower endorsement of the Protestant work ethic. Upper-middle-class Blacks had a higher belief in the work ethic than working-class or middle-class Blacks.[9] The authors' explanatory framework focused on social oppression as a key factor in shaping ethnic identity, such as racism, sexism, and classism that operate to temper enthusiasm for the work ethic, in lieu of the belief that hard work is solely enough to succeed.

In addition to their class and ethnic identity, I wanted to discern the siblings' attitudes and beliefs about welfare and how their ways of seeing comport with their attitudes and beliefs about self-efficacy and their fervent care ethics for "the least of these." Recognizing that humans are complex beings, the advantage of an in-depth interview, in contrast to a survey, is to allow individuals to make meaning of their own truth and to capture complex realities, rather than having individuals respond to an imposed set of social constructs. For how one feels, thinks, and behaves do not always align across space and time. To gain an understanding of these social phenomena, Lubertha, Roscoe Jr., Mary, and Debbie offered a window into their strong work orientation and how it accorded with ethnic and class identity, welfare, and the care ethics. Starting with Lubertha, she felt closer to poor and working-class Blacks. She affirmed Wayne's representation of their father's view of welfare, although she has "always felt those that need it [should get it], but we need to take care of our own." Lubertha further stated,

> While growing up, my father interpreted it differently. You were trying to get something for nothing. And that you were not a man if you could not take care of your family. As we got older, we understood there were legitimate reasons for welfare. But we grew up believing that men were the head of the house, even though now women run their own households. We have changed our minds on that, but we did not grow up feeling that way about welfare because it had a stigma that you could not take care of your family on your own, and the government controls you and that is the way Father looked at it. And my father took care of his own family.

Lubertha acknowledges that "there are certain legitimate reasons why people need welfare." Nevertheless, she also believes that "if you are well enough to work and you have no restrictions, you need to go to work. Do something if you are able to!" As one who toiled assiduously as an administrator for Elizabeth City State University, she interjected this personal reflection about work: "I worked for them with a conscience. I do not believe in just picking up a paycheck. I was conscious of what I was doing, and I had a little integrity. I wanted my school to do well: I wanted to represent my school well because it was an HBCU and things were not coming as easily as now. I have seen times where we really had to scratch [for money] to keep our children in school." When Lubertha had a stroke in 2013, her highly prized work ethic, which kept her in good standing with her employer, paid off in having a good health plan that covered her illness. Having firsthand knowledge of the impact of illness, she, along with her siblings, believes everyone should have some form of universal health care. Lubertha expresses what it means personally to have good employee benefits, resulting from her lengthy work history. "Having an excellent health plan has been a blessing to me and my family, so I don't become a burden to them, and I can help somebody else."

Self-sufficiency for herself, and for others, is a significant familial value. But it does not negate the neighborly care ethics transmitted by her parents:

> Whatever my father had in surplus, we were always driven to share it with the family that had less. He would take part of what he had and give it to them. We grew up doing that. Whatever we had in surplus, we had to share it. That is what he would do. Naturally, he wanted you to be about something. But if you did not have anything and you were

in his presence, you were going to have something. He was going to share what he had. And that was natural for us, and that is why I said the poor and working class.

Roscoe Jr. did not discuss his overt perspective on welfare; however, he described himself initially as feeling closer to the middle class, but upon further reflections, he stated, "I agree with Bertha [Lubertha] in identifying with the poor and unfortunate ones." Roscoe, who took over his father's construction business after his death, admitted,

I worked with my dad from a little boy, and he would hire these guys who were broken down and no one else wanted them. I would get mad. I said to my dad, "Hire somebody who is prepared or has his stuff together. Hire somebody who has a driver's license and a car that is ready to roll and is not broken." I said that I would never do that. To this day, I do the same thing that my father did. The ones in life that need a hand, I hold high. Do this to the least of these, you are doing it to me. I use a lot of the ones who are broken down, in need of some help, and a little push in life to sail through. My mom and dad did the same identical thing. I was so afraid they were going to take advantage of my dad. He would give them a whole day's pay for a half day's work. I would get so mad with Daddy. And lo and behold, I do the same thing today.

Mary admitted also to feeling closer to working-class Blacks. In explaining why she identified with working-class Blacks, Mary responded this way: "I know what Roscoe and Lubertha are saying, but I can't think poor. We had a store and my mom would cook there. Sometimes the migrant workers would come in, but they could not pay. But they still got a chance to eat. You need to have something to take it to that next level of helping others. I have to go with working-class Blacks for that reason." Mary's belief about welfare is remarkably similar to Lubertha's in that accountability and self-sufficiency do not rebut the care ethics.

"Even though Dad said, 'With my twelve, I will not participate in welfare,' we appreciated the pride that he had in taking care of his family," Mary said. "We were never on welfare, but we totally believe in the welfare system for those in dire need of it. Sometimes things just happen, and people drop to the bottom. People who really need it do not stay on it for very long. I would like for that cushion to be there. I believe in the system, but there are those who do take advantage of it."

Debbie's class and ethnic identity appeared somewhat more fluid. Initially, she stated, "I can identify with all of them. . . . [But] I chose working class for this reason: My father was always helping someone in need. I have a giving heart, and I do not mind helping someone less fortunate. It is a gift that I found I have, but I did not know I had." Hence, it is not surprising when Debbie remarked that welfare should be available "if you meet the requirements and are honest about it, you should have access. Let your conscience be your guide."

For the James siblings, having a strong work ethic does not appear to have any bearing on their ethnic or perceived class identity. Moreover, their perspective of welfare and their emphasis on being self-sufficient do not dampen their care ethics. For the biblical precept of caring for the "least of these," based on Matthew 25:40, is one of the James family's core principles and identity markers.

In turning to the issue of race in the subsequent section, this question is explored: How do the James siblings view and negotiate the societal constraints imposed by this important social axis?

### In the Eyes of God, We Are Equal

Bursting with a harvest of compassion, Samuel uttered these words as he spoke mindfully in an orotund voice, "If you are a homeless person sitting on the steps or a mayor, we treat everybody the same. My daddy would say that 'regardless of people's status, treat everybody the same. Respect everyone.' That comes from being rooted in Christ, and everyone has Him in his or her hearts."

"For in the eyes of God, we are all equal" is the credo of the James family. As the family sat around the table during dinners or during other family events, Pennie and Roscoe taught cherished life lessons about how their children should comport themselves in the presence of others. For instance, Wayne not only recalled Pennie's concern about the manner in which her offspring spoke to others, she also said, "When you talk with people, look them in the eyes. You don't talk at the floor or around them." Roscoe taught his sons to have respect for women. Samuel insisted, "My daddy never laid a hand on my mother. My daddy wanted respect for his daughters. When guys came to the house, they were afraid of my father since he was six feet five inches. He wanted the best for his daughters. My daddy never raised a hand at us, except once when he accidentally struck Wayne." Roscoe and Pennie also expected their daughters to respect themselves. Lubertha fervently recalled this saying of her father: "My father wanted us to be a lady. Father would say, 'Every woman can be a woman, but not every woman can be a lady.' We had to more or less prove that we were ladies before we could go certain places." Their parental advice still holds a powerful sway. As an example, Terri put forth this witty assertion: "My mama always told me if you want to have children, do it the right way. Be married! The fear she put in me is probably why I am not married and do not have children. I said, 'Mama, can you take this belt off me now? I am really getting older.'" Such gendered and general life lessons about morality and respect were the order of the day growing up in the James household. These life lessons precluded, however, specific teachings on race and racism. As Eric, and other siblings, consistently contended, "While growing up, there was not a lot of conversation about race. Whether it was work, school, church, or home, we were taught to treat everyone equally. In the Bible, it talks about loving your neighbors, not race or how to treat this person or that person. Everyone got fair treatment. We did not go deep into how society treated us or into Black and white. It was not a conversation in the house. We stood by everyone."

Race, though socially constructed, is a reality in our society, and like class and gender, it is one of its pivotal axes. Depending on your location in the racial hierarchy in this society, advantages and privileges accrue to members of the dominant racial group, while members of racially nondominant groups experience disadvantages. Given that race is a reality in our society, how do members of the James family perceive, experience, negotiate, and respond to race and racism? While growing up in Elizabeth City, North Carolina, what were their lived racial experiences in this small city? According to the siblings, the issue of race was not a central theme in their lives. In fact, their experiences with racism were practically nil. Since their perceptual views and experiential encounters differed significantly from the majority of African Americans similarly situated at that historical juncture, how do we account for such differences? To understand the chasm, the subsequent plausible explanations are advanced. Although the South has undergone major social and economic shifts over the last fifty years, this region of the country was well known for its overt racial segregation in policies, attitudes, and differential and often harsh treatments of Blacks, particularly in rural and small-town settings. But even during de jure segregation and immediately following the civil rights movement, the social and cultural milieu was neither totally Black nor white; it was sometimes shades of gray. Although complex and hierarchal, occasionally Blacks and whites formed deep emotional bonds between them. This was particularly true with Black women domestics who cleaned, cooked, nursed, and raised children for white families. It was also the case if individuals were viewed as having nonthreatening physical and social attributes, or if they were perceived as having desirable skill sets in which members of the dominant group derived benefits. As a result of this social bond, many individuals occupying this status were able to build social capital for themselves, their families, and their communities. Roscoe can serve as a case in point. He was perceived as honest, polite, and hardworking; hence, his good name became his calling card for his craft skills as a drywaller and plasterer, which were in great demand by his mostly white clients. Upon his death, his good name was still paying social capital dividends more than fourteen years later. The James family's home was being renovated by Roscoe Jr., so they needed temporary housing, and the owner of a building supply company in Elizabeth City, whom Roscoe Sr. had frequently interacted, came to their rescue. Lubertha gave this account of what took place: "One Sunday evening, Debbie, Mary, and I were returning to Karen's house after church service, and we passed this brick home with a long driveway and beautiful crepe myrtle trees. It had a handwritten sign 'For Rent' posted on the property near the mailbox. Admiring the house, we called right away, but there was no answer." At the time, they were unaware that the property belonged to the building supply owner until Wayne called the following day. "The rest of the story is history. After learning who the house inquirer was and the family needing it, [the building supply owner] did not hesitate [to lease it]. He was a blessing for three years," Lubertha stated. Samuel added the property was also leased far below its market value. More economically independent individuals like Roscoe were able to protect their children from the harsh realities of everyday racism. Furthermore, as the James siblings, particularly the older ones, were growing up in the late 1950s, 1960s, and 1970s, they benefited from the changing racial climate resulting from the modern civil rights movement and its continuance in the Black Power movement. Finally, since the James family's mission is to follow in the ethics of Jesus's footsteps, any negative racial contact may be perceived as general adversities of the human condition. These explanations may well account for their minimal encounters with racism and might help to explain why race has not been a salient focus of their lives. Here, in their own voices, they share their perspectives on race and racism, as well as their responses to any perceived racial prejudice and discrimination.

When the question about racial experience was posed to the four older siblings whom I interviewed separately from the other ones, Lubertha spoke first, noting, "In all my sixty-five years, I never remember having personal encounters that set us off." But she did remember, along with Debbie and Mary, these serial occurrences during elementary school. She had attended both a segregated elementary school and a segregated high school until the tenth grade. Here is what she observed: "The kids going to the white school on bus number 37 would always stick their fingers up as we walked along the road. Being focused on what Jesus was about, we did not retaliate or take it personally. We looked at them pitifully. Usually, we would have another adult walking along with their children. That is the only incident that I personally encountered." For Debbie, those memories are still vivid. "When we were in elementary school, I would always turn around and see bus number 37 and I would hate to see it coming because I knew they were going to stick their fingers up. It bothered me because I knew they were telling me to go to hell. I tried not to take it too personally. I said they were kids: They were taught to do that. I did not believe they were superior to us. We were taught to treat people equally."

Lubertha remembered when Elizabeth City had a separate white and Black hot dog stand and Black and white water fountains. She recalled, "The separation did not deter me, even though I was young, because we did not have to deal with it that much." Here are her reasons for feeling that way:

> We did not do a lot of socializing because Daddy was protective of where we were and what we were doing. In our community where we lived, my father was well respected and also my mother. The whites always seemed to respect my daddy. Although he had a lot of children, he was a self-skilled plasterer, and although there were not a lot of people doing that kind of work, the whites wanted that kind of work. So Dad was in and out of their homes rather often. We were taught in church that we were the same in God's eyes. We were not taught that we were less than. We were never taught to do anything against whites. My father and mother taught us to respect the way Jesus lived. And so, we basically loved on them whether they loved on us or not. Most of the time, my mother had a day job working for white families. She came into contact with one white family that owned a wholesale product company, and this man was very kind to her and our family. If we ever needed anything, they told us to let them know. We fell in their favor, not that we were kissing up. We were considered religious, and we did not step outside the line. We knew that we all have faults as well. That was how we conducted ourselves. As far as racism affecting me, it did not have a big effect on me because I was taught to turn the other cheek.

Modeling the life of Christ called for the James family to turn the other cheek when faced with adversities. This ideal was the guiding force in their adaptive response to racism. But even for the true believer, a breaking point can happen. That moment came for Karen in the 1980s while working as a waitress in an Elizabeth City's grocery with a café. She vividly recalled this incident: "When I asked the gentleman, 'May I help you?' he said, 'I don't want the [n word] to serve me.' I grabbed a pair of tongs to pick up the chicken breast and I threw it at him." The disruptive customer was ordered to leave the restaurant. After regaining her composure, she did not interpret or internalize that scenario as personal. After all, like the rest of the siblings, she learned "in the eyes of God, we are all equal." It was the first time Karen had shared this incident with seven of her siblings whom I interviewed separately from the four oldest on the issue of race, class, and gender. A spontaneous, nervous laughter erupted following Karen's surprise revelation, perhaps because it did not follow their customary tradition of turning the other cheek. When Samuel shared Karen's story with the four older siblings whom I later interviewed on the topic of race and racism, Lubertha speculated, "I think Karen never shared that story because she did not want Dad to know that she retaliated."

Even though Lubertha indicated that racism did not have a major impact on her and the immediate family, as she grew older she became more aware of its impact on those outside the family.

> It really did not have a great impact on me until I started getting older and I could see what other Black people were going through. I would hear my classmates talk about what was happening in the family and in the community, or hear about somebody burning a cross in the community, or somebody said the n word. But that was something that I was spared in my sixty-five years, and I thank the Lord that I was spared. But I still empathized with classmates and those on the bus talking about it. There were just certain communities that you did not want to be in after darkness. There were certain places that we were not allowed to go, so we were protected by just not being there. We could not socialize like other children. We could not go to basketball games until we were in our late teens. [Racism] was going on around us, but we were sort of protected from that. We knew that we could only act a certain way and that was how we were going to behave. I do thank the Lord for that strong family background, but in a way, it kind of made us feel like we were missing something.

Never having faced racism in Elizabeth City, Samuel certainly had missed something until he was blindsided by his first racial epithet while "jogging along a roadside in the vicinity of NASA and a [white] boy around thirteen years old called me the n word." Likewise, Terri, too, had not experienced its sting until she and a friend were driving along a road and some white men hollered out the n word while passing them. Neither Samuel nor Terri internalized the derogatory word. Now, prior to Samuel's run-in with the racially disparaging name-calling near NASA, he reported only positive encounters in his hometown. Having attended an integrated elementary school and high school while growing up with what he described as a "good mix of Black and white students," he remembered,

> It was fifty-fifty Black and white. The guidance counselor, a white female, was very supportive and my seventh grade teacher, a white female, was very supportive. We had a diverse group of students. We had Asians, Native Americans, etc. I did not experience racism when I was in school. I would go to dinner and spend the night with my white friends. I never experienced anything really major other than seeing it on the news and hearing other people talk about it. Mom never really talked about it nor Daddy. They both had close white friends that they saw on a regular basis. They respected my father very well.

When I inquired about the perception of Samuel's experience vis-à-vis other Black males in and outside the classroom, he remarked, "It was the same in the classroom, but I don't know about outside it. I was not with them. But I know that people are scarred by racism."

Eric was startled by his first encounter with racism but not scarred. Having lived by the family's creed of "treating everybody as equal," it was unsettling for him when he left home for college and stumbled blindly into his first racial incident:

> I can talk about one incident that I experienced while growing up as an educated Black man. I learned more about race when I left home at seventeen and the way I was treated by other ethnicities based on how I looked. I was frustrated. I did not talk to my parents about it. I talked to other people about it to calm me down a bit. I was with my brother Wayne the first couple of years in college. As a young Black man, I lived in a big house with lots of roommates near a predominantly white college. When I stepped out of the car, I got stopped by the police and I was not even in my car. The white police officer asked, "What are you doing in this area?" And it shocked me because I never had an encounter with a policeman. I never had a big issue with race in high school. I never experienced anything like that. I told him I lived there

and pointed to him where I lived. He asked for my license and registration, and I was not even in my vehicle. I had what he wanted. I kept my cool, and I gave him what he wanted. That was my early struggle, and it was kind of shocking. I was frustrated and I had to walk it off. But that was my biggest problem. I knew to be careful and have what he needed. I did not act a certain way or question him. It was the law enforcement. As a Black man, I had never felt judged and never have gone through anything like that until I got to college.

Once again, in his position as educator and student support counselor, Eric felt judged as a Black man. Always dressed sartorially correct in his neatly pressed suit and tie, he behaved as the consummate professional. Hence, he was shocked and taken aback by the nuances of gendered racism expressed by his white principal who felt too many girls surrounded him. Having taken care of his father at thirteen and having lived with eight sisters, not only did he gain considerable foresight into understanding the psychology of women, but he also developed a keen empathetic and nurturing spirit, critical attributes for his position as student support counselor. In fact, his people skills were the primary reason for being hired at his jobsite.

William E. Cross, in his revised Nigrescence model, identified individuals like Eric as exhibiting a low salience for race in the pre-encounter stage. However, when he experienced his initial encounter with the police, he entered the encounter stage.[10] After his initial shock, Eric understood he was treated differently based solely on his physical characteristics. It resulted in his increased awareness about what it means to be a Black male in this society. However, his creed of treating everyone the same, which is based on his religious orientation, remained more salient.

Like Lubertha, Mary and Debbie indicated they never had anyone hurl a vocal racial label at them. In fact, they have lived lives absent of any racial encounters except for bus 37 episodes in elementary school. Shirley expressed similar feelings as her older sisters. For she, as all the siblings, internalized the family's motto of the importance of treating everyone equally. With this shared familial perspective, intended or unintended racial acts might not be as easily recognized as such, or they might be reinterpreted. Mary summed up this somewhat color-blind outlook, when she stated, "I don't remember [race] being discussed because my parents said we are all born from the same God. We were never taught to be prejudiced against anyone because of race, creed, color, or culture. I will say that a few of us dated outside the race, but there was never any fear of bringing that person home. And that was what our parents taught us. There were no limitations on race because we are one race but different colors." Darlene, an administrator in a federal agency, also espoused a parallel view. However, when she confronted an insidious form of racism, the everyday microaggression of being invalidated and ignored by her white colleague, she turned the other cheek. She kept speaking continuously to her colleague who refused to return her civility. Eventually, after recognizing she "preferred not to speak," Darlene ceased doing so and just delivered her work to the coworker. Darlene kept the *Daily Word* on her desk and read it on her breaks. This daily office scenario occurred for ten years. When the white colleague became extremely ill and had a deathbed awakening, it led to a "change of heart after she returned to work." For the first time after ten years, she spoke to Darlene. Moreover, she remembered Darlene's reading of the *Daily Word* and desired to know more about it. She presented Darlene with a figurine gift, which Darlene graciously accepted and kept on her desk. Eventually, they became good friends. Like Karen's story, no one had heard Darlene's. When Samuel retold Darlene's account to the older siblings, Lubertha said, "I rest my case. As Daddy would say, 'No cross, no crown.' Even though I never heard that story, it does not surprise me. We were taught to continue to do 'good.' And Daddy would say, 'Do not complain because if you give up in times of adversity, your faith is small.'"

"I experienced the same thing when I moved to a white neighborhood in 2001," Roscoe Jr. claimed upon hearing Darlene's account. It stirred his memories of a similar incident. Sometimes painful memories of old racial ghosts are buried deeply in the subconscious mind and lay dormant until reawakened by some stimulus, a common pattern that I observed in my previous research. Here is Roscoe's anecdote of the uncivil neighbor:

A neighbor across the street was very prejudice. My mom and daddy instilled in us, "Don't belabor people back the same." My mom had one Scripture that she imparted to all: "Be not overcome with evil; overcome evil with good." That transcended all of us. When I would speak to the neighbor, at first I got roiled up, but then I went back to what my parents instilled in us. And then I went back to the Scripture, and I got angry inside. But I prayed about it. And the second year, I kept on speaking. It continued for three years, four years, five years, and six years. At one point, I said that I shall not speak to him anymore. Then something inside of me remembered what Bertha [Lubertha] said, "No cross, no crown." One day, I had to go to Garland, North Carolina, to give a eulogy. As I was getting in my truck, I said I was not going to speak to him. God is my witness in heaven I said that to myself. Then a small quiet voice told me to speak. I spoke. And for the first time in seven years, he spoke back to me. This was in 2005. It reminded me of the big chip of ice; you keep chipping with love. Naturally, I wanted to give up, but God said keep on showing love. To this day, he speaks to me every day.

Our parents were our mentors and tutors. We got it from home. We have been accepted, and we have triumphed over [adversities]. Sometimes we struck out. Beyond our flaws, we picked up and carried on the cross. We used that philosophy today. About 80 percent of my business is white. Daddy's business was mostly white.

Whether the topic at hand is racism or respect, the ethical teachings of Jesus are interwoven into the lives of the James family and into their discourses. With faith and family forming the foundational framework, the siblings have quilted threads of their core values into a commemorative keepsake to pass to the next generation. In telling the story of the James family, the significance of codifying strong family values to transmit to future generations has become clearer. Perhaps in the same way, it became clearer when Lubertha was listening to other siblings speak during an interview regarding their father's testifying. It was his way of codifying. During her epiphany, here is what Lubertha opined: "When I heard them [siblings] talking, I understand why he had to do what he did because we are a living testimony that God can keep not just a small family but a large family together always. They don't have to be in the street, to be locked up, or to be dependent on public assistance. God can take care of His own. I know that for a fact. It is God's blessings."

Lubertha's revelatory moment about her father's testimony bears witness to the importance of remembrance, an idea as old as the book of Deuteronomy 4:9: "Do not forget the things your eyes have seen or let them slip from your heart as long as you live. Teach them to your children and your children's children." Now that the James siblings have told their family story of what binds them, with Lubertha having the last say, a world of wisdom is embedded in their family narrative for future generations that is so worthy of remembering.

In turning to the next generation, the offspring of the siblings and the grandchildren of Roscoe and Pennie James, the question at hand is, what do they remember? Are they heeding the timeless lesson of Deuteronomy 32:7—"Remember the days of old; consider the generations long past. Ask your father and he will tell you, your elders, and they will explain to you"?

## CHAPTER SIX

# Binding the Good Name through Linking the Generational Chain

> If you don't recount your family history, it will be lost. Honor your
> own stories and tell them too. The tales may not seem very important,
> but they are what binds families and makes each of us who we are.
>
> —MADELEINE L' ENGLE

Symbolizations inherent in stories that bind families serve essential functions
of reinforcing moral messages, consolidating identity, and linking generations. For these reasons, I asked Candace, Chad, Mary Ashley, and Paige, the
grandchildren of Pennie and Roscoe, if they were familiar with their grandfather's legacy of having a "good name." Although they never heard it, a rich
vein of values coursed through their interview of January 27, 2018, linking the
generational chain. As the descendants of Mary Magdalene, Chad and Mary
Ashley grew up in Atlanta, Georgia, and so did Candace and Paige, the
children of Shirley. Yet, despite their geographical separation from their an-
cestral home in Elizabeth City, North Carolina, and their unfamiliarity with
Roscoe's legacy, I found the good name there in the progenies' heritage of
faith, family, noble character, respect, empowerment, strong work ethic,
service, and optimism. Here, Jodi Picoult, an American writer, aptly reminds
us, "Just because you didn't put a name to something, did not mean it wasn't
there." For indeed, their values bore the mark of their grandfather Roscoe Sr.,
although at the time of his death in 2000, his grandchildren were too young to
remember very much about him. As Candace remarked, "I really had only
one memory of my grandfather and that is when he had Parkinson's disease. I
did not really have a chance to have a conversation with him, but I felt his
impact through my mom, aunts, and uncles."

Many cultural critics of present-day family life argue older generations
have lost their sway in instilling familial values and beliefs in millennials of
Candace's cohort. It appears especially to be the case in a postmodern society characterized by globalization, polarization, technology, rampant individualism, familial mobility and instability, in addition to other innumerable
social and economic forces. Hence, it is a testament to the strength of the
James family that elements of their core values are strongly fused into the

grandchildren's social being. Like the James siblings, two of their fundamental values—faith and family togetherness—are inextricably bound. Family studies show that the transmission of religious tenets and values across generations is one of the major means of maintaining connection within the family. Casey E. Copen and Merril Silverstein noted that despite the growth in secularism and the expansion of alternative spiritual movements that value self-fulfillment and religious expression over conventionality, the influence of grandparents in transmitting religious beliefs to their grandchildren is still strong.[1] Likewise, in a longitudinal study examining the transmission of three dimensions of religiosity—religious service attendance, religiousness, and religious ideology across generations from 1971 to 2000, the researchers found, despite weakening ties in grandparents' influence in service attendance and the strengthening of their influence in conservative religious beliefs, grandparents still had an impact on all three dimensions of religiosity independent of parents. This continuing influence suggests religious beliefs and practices fashioned within nuclear and extended families continue into later stages of the life cycle with both parents and grandparents acting independently and mutually as vital religious social agents.[2]

In extrapolating the literature review on intergenerational transmission of religiosity, much support is found for its contribution to higher family functioning and enhanced family relations.[3] This connection was evident in the responses of Pennie and Roscoe's grandchildren. "Family orientation is important to me and being together no matter what is really important," noted Paige. According to Chad, "Growing up, I learned values from my large family, and I learned that we should be connected. I am connected to my father's side as well." Although Chad chafed at his mother's demands that he remains connected to God, he has stayed steadfast. "Mom got on my nerves, but she always said, 'Be connected to the man above.' I don't go to church as much as I need to, but I have learned to be connected with the man above." Seemingly more imbued with a vernal freshness toward religiosity, Candace readily admitted, "One of my values is faith. I got a lot of my development and faith through my mom and the James side of the family. This is what has gotten me through life because I have experienced a lot of hardships. And if you have faith, all things are possible through God."

"Love Christ, love God, pray, and show compassion for everyone regardless of their background," says Paige. Her avowal is an expression of her faith, but it also embodies the values of her nuclear and extended family. Such ethical conviction has helped to shape her beliefs about being of service to others, maintaining respect for others, and having noble character.

Growing up, I always felt that Christianity was the official religion of the family. We heard lots of stories from the Bible, and my mom would tell us about a lot of things happening out in the world. I was taught to believe that we should treat each other how we want to be treated. I also feel like we should show compassion to people. We should take the initiative to understand one another before it results in violence, hatred, or judgment. I think that was built into the church we went to, and that was mostly a Baptist church we went to for a while. I think that is where I came to understand this really is an important thing. So I feel it is a mixture between my going to church and my mom and dad.

For Paige, "showing compassion is a universal value." It is what she observed not only from her religion but also from her aunts and uncles. "Helping someone is the natural thing to do. There is no hierarchy: we are all the same. We are not less than anybody else. I have observed that in church, and that is one of its ideals." When individuals espouse compassion but do not practice it, she is discomforted by the discrepancy. "I see politicians, like Donald Trump, who extol these values but practice greed. I struggle with him stereotyping people and showing discrimination. He is white, and white men are at the top. Being privileged, and the way you see the world, is literally a difference between helping and not helping."

Like Paige, Candace echoed similar sentiments about her sense of empathy when she stated, "I have a strong sense of compassion for others. I find myself wanting to help people as much as I can." And so does Chad, who acknowledged that his kindheartedness is fueled by his family and his spiritual undergirding:

I get my compassion from my mother. She puts a lot of time into church. She does maintenance and lots of work until late at night. She gets a lot of peace out of doing it. And you cannot argue with that. She also helps members out at her church with anything that needs doing. I know I got that from my mother. Sometimes, she is taken advantage of when it comes to being compassionate. I am taken advantage of also, but it is not going to change me. My friends know that I will help them out. In the end, God knows my heart. I feel good when I help people out, whether they are taking advantage of me or not. I get a good feeling, whether it is giving a homeless person a couple of dollars or whatever it is, I know that I have helped somebody out. I know that when I was growing up, I did not have a lot and I had to struggle, so I can get a feel from where they are coming.

While growing up, Paige remembered visiting the extended family in Elizabeth City, North Carolina, during holidays. Memory was busy at her heart as she vividly recalled the impact of family gatherings, where compassion was outwardly manifested, as well as the ritual of prayer. "I would say that I adopted prayer from my mom's values. Maybe the ultimate way of resolving conflict is to pray about it. With prayer, there is the sense that you have somewhere to always turn and you are not dealing alone with things yourself, which is another aspect of the [James side of the family] that is reflected in me, and it is what everyone has already said."

Not unlike the James siblings, the entwinement of faith and family formed the foundation of Pennie and Roscoe's grandchildren's ideals, values, and norms. Mary Ashley, a college student, would agree with that assessment, but she would add that the embracement of an empowering optimism came from observing the actions of her mother, along with having her feet straddled between the two institutions.

> Being dedicated, my mom showed me a lot through watching her, especially when my mom lost her job. They were laying off people at her job, and unfortunately, she was one of those they let go. For two years, she could not find a job and she ended up working at a voting poll, which was paying minimum wage. She stayed persistent and dedicated to finding a job. I rarely saw her break down or cry. She just prayed about it. But she knew God would bless her with a new job, and He did. Often, we have struggled financially, but my mom showed me how dedication is important, especially with my being in school and in maintaining my grades. It was a struggle for me, but I always stayed dedicated even though I was not always getting the grades I wanted. I wanted an A, but I was getting a B. I was trying my hardest.

For Mary Ashley, "the only real failure in life is not trying. I have had a lot of disappointments. I have wanted a job very badly, but I did not get it. It is discouraging, but if I did not try, I would not have ever known. Failure is a part of life. It will forever be a part of my life because through failure, you reach success." Mary Ashley finds not only comfort in her sense of empowerment through resilience that is derived from the faith absorbed from her mother, but she also feels a sense of well-being that emanates from the enmeshment in a strong nuclear and extended familial support system.

> My mother is a great support system. Being supportive is a great value. The James family has the best support system that I've ever witnessed.

We are all here for one another. If we have a problem, we always have each other. When my grandfather passed, I witnessed the most support from my family. And I can go to any aunt, uncle, cousin, or grandparent and I can ask them anything, or if I need anything, they will be there for me. Unfortunately, a lot of my friends struggle with support from their fathers. I have my father, and my cousins have their fathers. My mom, aunts, and uncles have all had their father in their lives. It is completely different from my friends; they never had their fathers in their lives. I can't really sympathize because my father has always been in my life. It has been a luxury to me compared to my friends. A lot of my friends are not close to their cousins, aunts, and uncles in the way we are. They don't spend as much time as I do with my family. They do not see their aunts or uncles until they pass on or they go to a funeral. So they are not as family-oriented as I am. I spend time with Candace and Paige and I spend time with my uncles outside of family events. I am glad to have my family and to be connected with them. I am appreciative of having that connection. I think it has to do with balance. Often in families, people seemed to be judgmental within the family and that breaks the family apart, which I have witnessed a lot. [Our family members] are not coming from a judgmental place; they are here to help you. They stick with the family, and that's the way they live.

Mary Ashley's pronouncement that her nuclear and extended family members live according to their ideals illustrates the truism that camaraderie, positive emotional support, and interaction within families are more likely to contribute to the transmission of those core values across generations. Douglas L. Flor and Nancy Flanagan Knapp identified parental behavior, for example, as an important factor in transmitting religious values to adolescents.[4] Like the James siblings, the grandchildren also perceived that a high degree of consistency exists between religious and ethical ideals and behaviors within their large extended family. Thus, it stands to reason why they value faith and family, along with noble character, respect, service, and the sense of empowerment undergirding those religious and ethical principles. In their fount of family values, add a sense of optimism to the transmission of beliefs. Its abundance overflows, and it is what Candace treasures about the James family—its optimism, joy, and humor.

Laughter is what I got from the family. They have a crazy sense of humor. And there is a lot of laughter when they get together. My grandparents were very strict, and it was a release for them to connect and bond over a whole lot of stories. But I also know some things they have experienced. They have become such great people with personable characteristics. You rarely see them in a bad mood. I try to make things lighthearted, although I am a serious person. But when I am around them, it makes things more lighthearted. When the family is together, you don't have any worries or cares and you just have fun.

Paige agreed with Candace with regard to how the family is easily moved to gaiety. She volunteered this comment: "Always when we are together, it is extremely light and there is no conflict or argument. There is a lot of dancing and fun. Fun is a huge value."

Seemingly, being in the presence of the James family is like spreading sunshine in the room. Hence, it is unsurprising when Chad aptly summed up Candace's, Paige's, and Mary Ashley's feelings about family in this way: "It is a blessing to have a family, and sometimes I like to bring friends around my family. The James family accepts everybody. Everybody hangs out with one another, not just with specific family members. It is just a blessing to be born into a family like that. I will carry on when I have my children like my grandparents did with their children." He opined that in the absence of material wealth and technology, the focus of his grandparents was more relational:

The cohesiveness of family has to do with my [grandparents] not having as much as we do, and it was easier to keep the family together. Technology has a lot to do with it. Kids are playing video games and on their phones. It is the times that we are in now. I always said I was going to do the same things for my children the way my mother did for me. When I have my children, they will be born into newer technology and they will have the technology, but I have to be creative. I will have my children spending more time outside instead of having them so dependent on technology. When I was young, I was always outside playing with my cousins or my friends. I will have my kids outside playing and having physical interactions with other kids and not being on the phone, in the house watching television, or isolating themselves behind closed doors.

The quintessential motif of family and faith runs deep within the generational triad. It is so pronounced that Corey, the son of Karen, requested to be interviewed after reading a draft of the James siblings' story. As a performer on the Disney Cruise Line, his global travels did not permit an in-depth interview. He did respond, however, to a questionnaire sent in May 2019. When asked, how did reading the family story impact him personally? here is what he wrote: "I knew that our family history went deep, and so much of who I am today is thanks to so many of my ancestors. Even though most of them are gone today, our bond, and the love that was established so long ago, is still alive and well in 2019. Seeing it on paper and reading someone else's take from outside of the family felt refreshing." On an emotional level, Corey felt this way:

Reading about my granddad, whom I don't remember at all [because]
I think he died when I was two and knowing his legacy already,
I couldn't help but feel proud, knowing that I come from such a
generous, charismatic, and respectable man. I definitely appreciate
and understand how lucky I am to come from such a dynamic family.
Some kids just don't get this type of love.

Prior to attending college in New York, Corey stated he lived with extended family, and he is still in touch, despite his schedule. "Now that I've graduated and I travel for my career, it's becoming a little more difficult. I try to call my mom at least four times a week and to talk with my grandmother, aunts, and uncles probably once a month. With social media today, we keep each other updated. And if they haven't heard from me in a while, they'll call me until I answer." When I asked Corey about the importance of knowing stories about his grandparents, mother, aunts, and uncles, he responded in this manner:

Knowing what they had to go through to be where they are today and
to be the amazing people that they are, I don't take opportunities
and rights with a grain of salt. Knowing that my grandparents,
uncles, and aunts had to break down tons of barriers (some of my
aunts and uncles even defying some of my grandparents' rules) to be
where they are now, I am very driven about what I want out of life and
what I want to contribute to this world. Carrying on the legacy is a
huge underlying reason why I do what I do and who I am. Yes, my
family is gigantic, so we are bound to have our different dynamics, and
one is not like the other. Yet what ties us together is love. Love that we
don't limit only within the family, but that spreads and deeply impacts
each stranger we meet. It's in our blood.

With a mild triumph in his tone, Corey affirmed the influence of his family: "My family has made me so much stronger, and much gentler, loving, and caring. I'm a family man. [It] makes me want to have my own family one day." Cherishing the notable characteristics of honesty, generosity, kindness, and love instilled by family will assist him in sustaining and building a resilient one of his own. "The very first thing my mother taught me was to be honest. Growing up and learning the hard way, I can say that honesty is the best policy, even if you're in the wrong." Corey felt the same about generosity and how important it is to "give, give, and give. My family is so selfless and never second-guesses when someone needs a hand. They are always willing to lend a helping hand." For Corey, it is also paramount to "be loving. Allow kindness to lead everything you do in this life. Whether personal, work, or whatever it may be, do it all out of love because then it becomes something more than just for you. Love is not shallow; you won't find it on the surface. It comes from a place much deeper."

In addition to having noble character, Corey views effective communication, which is vital to respect, as crucial. He noted that "within a family, you will have some disagreements and differences of opinion. [But] be open to conversation." Being empowered and having a strong work ethic are additional core values. He remarked, "Success won't come easy, and no one is going to hand it to you. You have to go out and be willing to grab it and own it. Obstacles will stand in your way, but you keep trudging through until you reach your goals. Stay on your grind." Here is what Corey heard from family members regarding his work ethic: "I have been told by [a lot of my family that I remind them] of my granddad and that we share a lot of the same habits and mannerisms. I definitely work like he did. Once I've started, I won't stop until it's done. I always want to give quality and not quantity. It's about what goes into the work." The impact of familial transmission of values is undeniably in Corey. "I feel like I didn't have a choice. They were all ingrained into me at a young age. They were already there."

In examining the values of Gabriel and Senya, the son and daughter of Samuel, it seems that Pennie and Roscoe's familial values are also deeply embedded in them, as revealed by their responses from a questionnaire administered in May 2019. By the time of its distribution, Gabriel and Senya were familiar with their grandfather's story, but they had not read their father's and his siblings' account of the family's collective narrative. Not surprisingly, faith and family prevailed once more as governing ideals in their young lives, even though like most teenagers in our society, sixteen-year-old Gabriel and thirteen-year-old Senya revel in typical cultural activities of their age cohort, such as hanging out with friends, participating in sports, playing video games, and going to school. Take this example as an illustration of their faith. When the question was asked about their favorite biblical narrative, Gabriel liked the story of David and Goliath and Senya admired the account of Moses leading the Israelites out of Egypt and crossing the Red Sea. Both stories embody faith, a key value in the familial socialization process. For Senya, her faith is reinforced in church attendance, which provides hope as well as an opportunity to spend time with family. And for Gabriel, church attendance is a "time to hear the Scriptures" and to find valuable lessons for living. Their ideals and practices are buttressed by their father and extended members of the James clan. Even the spirit of their grandfather Roscoe still hovers nearby. Even though Gabriel and Senya were born many years after his death, they are familiar with stories about his legacy. For Gabriel, it is how his grandfather successfully raised twelve children, his strong work ethic as a plasterer, and his great character. For Senya, it is her remembrance of grandfather "always putting family first."

Specifically, their father, Samuel, whom Gabriel admires as being "strong, resilient, faithful, polite, respectful, understanding, and peaceful," has not only instilled the values of faith and family, but he has also taught him to be respectful of his parents, "to be a gentleman, to treat others as you would want them to treat you, and to do your best at everything you do." His extended network of aunts and uncles has also encouraged him to "keep pushing forward, no matter what has happened, and to keep doing great work." Whereas Gabriel captures a more nuanced masculine side of his father Samuel, Senya respects his trustworthiness, supportiveness, and self-assurance, but she also admires her father's softer side of "forgiveness, kindness, honesty," and lovingness. Having a wealth of empathy, it is not surprising why Samuel has constantly reinforced to both of his children how essential it is "to help people in need and to look at others' point of view." Samuel's siblings, whom Senya admires for their "enthusiasm, humor, dependability, and success," have bolstered those views. Additionally, a more salient lesson that she has internalized from aunts and uncles is that "sometimes you have to let go, forgive, and forget." Hence, when Senya was asked to rank five values in order of importance to her, forgiveness was among them as well as family, friends, honesty, and loyalty. Caring for others, respecting others, and treating them equally are also essential principles for Senya. Her deeds are matched by her ideals. Senya affirmed that she "volunteers to help the homeless" and she offers support to "friends through rough times."

Gabriel, like Senya and Pennie and Roscoe's other grandchildren, carries with him the James family's trilogy of faith, family, and noble character. The last includes dedication, friendship, honesty, and love. An added value is his promising work ethic in which he expressed being happier spending time working during summer vacation than not working. Having a strong work ethic is more likely to fuel one's sense of empowerment. Hence, when Gabriel was asked to choose between the following two statements—"I think parents should be financially responsible for their children until at least thirty" or "I think parents should encourage their children to be financially independent immediately after completion of high school if they do not attend college"—he chose the latter. Desiring independence is also critical to the process of empowerment. Along with Gabriel's developing strong work ethic, a sense of empowerment and independence, an ethic of care, service, and generosity has been bestowed on him. It has impacted his idea of success, which is "accomplishing a goal no matter how small or big." Gabriel, who plans to study computer engineering after high school, is interested in being successful, but he is also more desirous of helping others like his friends than becoming rich with myriads of material and financial resources. Like Senya, he is also interested in helping the homeless by sharing his monetary resources. Even as a young boy, he would ask his father for a dollar to give to the homeless. Interestingly, Michael Bond, in the *New Scientist*, presents research by Dacher Keltner at the University of California, Berkeley, and his colleagues on the link between wealth and empathy. The researchers found more empathy toward others among individuals with less resources than those with greater resources. Keltner reasoned that if individuals are experiencing difficult times, they are more likely to need the help of others in overcoming their plight. As a result, they are more likely to develop greater sensitivity to the feelings and needs of those in their milieu. It is important, however, to be mindful of drawing rigid conclusions about the wealthier as having less empathy, especially since most of the studies were conducted in a laboratory with college students and not in real life.[5]

In examining the James family's values, beliefs, and attitudes across generations, what emerged is a consensual solidarity. A wealth of noble character, empathy, generosity, kindness, and compassion—along with faith, family, respect, strong work ethic, service, empowerment, and optimism—is evidenced in varying degrees among individuals and across generations, supporting the notion of continued reproduction of the social capital and social values inherited from Pennie and Roscoe. Although education was not emphasized by the grandchildren, one can assume its importance as promoted by Pennie. Except for Gabriel and Senya, who are honor students in school, the other five grandchildren interviewed for this book are attending college or have graduated from college and are now pursuing their career goals. For example, Candace, who completed Georgia Tech in 2011 with a BS in computer science, is cofounder and CEO of Techturized Inc., a high-tech hair care company based in Atlanta, Georgia. Her consumer brand, Myavana, is a personalized hair care service that recommends products and services based on scientific analysis of the consumer's hair type and texture. She has been named on WWD's Top Fifty Beauty Innovators under forty, 2016 Forbes thirty under thirty list in the category of retail and e-commerce, and BET's Next in Class STEM Award Winner. Her company has been featured nationally on CNN, Headline News, BuzzFeed, *The Real* daytime talk show, *Marie Claire* magazine, MSNBC's *Melissa Harris-Perry* show, *Essence* magazine, *Ebony* magazine, Black Enterprise, and Business Insider. In 2019, she was a featured speaker at the Essence Festival and traveled to Uganda to assist young entrepreneurs. Others are on their way in reproducing the social capital transmitted by Pennie and Roscoe as well as expanding their cultural and economic capital while upholding the Jameses' good name.

## Talking Race and Gender in the Third Generation

Although the social capital transmitted to Pennie and Roscoe's grandchildren has been expanded and reproduced by them, race and gender sometimes collide to constrain social capital resources and thus life chances. Rochelle Parks-Yancey, utilizing a nationally representative sample, examined the impact of race, gender, and social capital resources on two career measures—earnings and promotions. Parks-Yancey found African Americans experienced a social capital deficit relative to whites and that men's and whites' career advantages accrued over time, while African American disadvantages amassed.[6] With the understanding that race and gender are pivotal realities in this society, how do the grandchildren differ from prior generations in attitudes, behaviors, and beliefs regarding these social forces? How do they negotiate race and gender?

Ostensibly, while the third generation shares core values with their parents and grandparents, including the idea of treating everyone the same, a noticeable shift occurred in their understanding, awareness, and acknowledgment of the impact of gender and race. With reference to gender, while caring for others is still paramount, more emphasis is on self-care because of the third generation's greater understanding of the burden of women's dual role in managing career and family. In addition, the third generation seems to have greater awareness of the restraining influence of race and gender and, in general, appears more comfortable in discoursing about the effects of the intersectionality of both on less powerful members of society. Take Paige, for example; she identifies with "being a woman first, and then being an African American." Without much prompting or probing, Paige, a senior in college at the time of the interview but now a recent college graduate, remarked how the impact of race and gender has both hindered and benefited her:

> Race and gender have both hurt and helped me. Growing up in the South is different because patriarchy is stronger. Being a woman, we look to men for direction. We overly extend ourselves and do not put ourselves first. We need to incorporate self-care first. Women want to help everyone else, which is good, but we fall short of taking care of ourselves.
>
> As far as African Americans, it is challenging. I think like James Baldwin who said to be African American is to be in a state of rage all the time. I sort of go in and out of stages of rage and disappointment. You want people to recognize African Americans for what we are. We are valuable for what we are. We are smart. We are not less than. We are just as capable as the next person. When institutions incorporate racism, it is tricky. It is like loving your history but trying to prove to people your value. We are just as valuable as the white man and just as capable. Recently, since Trump became president, I have become numbed because I simply cannot believe that his rhetoric is so racist. If we are not being painted in the best light, they are saying something about minorities. It is also beautiful because there is light in struggle. It brings us together. Sometimes I think we could organize a little more, but it has brought us together. There is more room for improvement. It has also brought other minorities together, and people want to be more active and organized. It has made us talk about race in class and beyond.

Paige negotiates the obstacles of race and gender in this way: "Believe in yourself and follow your dream. Allow for change and discomfort." Mary Ashley, a college student and a photographer, agrees with Paige that gender plays a more significant role in her life than race. Knowing her value is Paige's way of managing and resisting the impact of gender and race.

> Gender usually has more of an effect on me, since photography is a boys' club, so to speak. I work with a male in photography, and I struggle to gain clients. Some people like me better and others like him better. Even though they tell me they like my work, they still go with my partner. They are saying I prefer you as a shooter, but I have

to go on as a second shooter. He will get paid more than I will. That is also the struggle of being a Black woman in America, as we are the least respected. Although I may take it to heart for that moment, I have to know and understand my value. I have to draw the line and move myself from partnering with him all the time to see if I can [make it]. Women have always had to prove themselves twice as much as a man does. As a Black woman, it is four times as much as a white man or a white woman. I have to work ten times harder and be better. You have to work twenty times harder as the next man. It bothers me, but I have to value myself and know my worth.

Although Mary Ashley's brother Chad claims that he has not experienced race or gender discrimination, he supports her assertion that "lots of males get more opportunities than women," but women "should have the same opportunities as well." Since Mary Ashley does not see herself as having similar life chances, she deals with the impact of race and gender by being excellent and working hard, along with valuing herself and knowing her worth. Chad, who is oriented toward positivity, would add, "Anything that is negative, you can make a positive out of it. Keep faith in God and things will work out. Be positive with everything you do." Candace, like Chad, has adopted an optimistic view. She prefers to deemphasize race as a reality of her existential being.

The more we talk about race and gender, it affects our consciousness, and God never intends us to live in a constant state of suffering. God intends for us to have abundance in our lives, and when we are not experiencing abundance, we can truly experience lack. I have come from a place of lack and it influences our belief system. If we are not conscious of that, we can go throughout life believing that we are lacking. Those beliefs affect our thoughts and behaviors. God has intended us to experience abundance financially, mentally, physically, and emotionally. I am really thankful for that. And so, I am focused on Christ who died for us so we can experience life more abundantly. I am focusing on me and my expectation to transfer abundance into my family, my community, and to my generation. I think we are the generation that can start to change that [place of lack] because we are more liberated in every phase of our lives.

In every generation, change is expected, desired, and undesired, so how important is it to maintain continuity between generations? Is the answer epitomized in writer Gail Lumet Buckley's declaration? She speculates that "family faces are magic mirrors. Looking at people who belong to us, we see the past, present, and future. We make discoveries about ourselves and them."[7] Or does the answer come closer to writer Pearl S. Buck? She pens, "The lack of emotional security of our American young people is due, I believe, to their isolation from the large family unit. No two people—no mere father and mother—as I have often said, are enough to provide emotional security for a child. He needs to feel himself one in a world of kinfolk, persons of variety in age and sex and temperament, and yet allied to himself by an indissoluble bond which he cannot break if he would, for nature has welded him into it before he was born."[8] The aforementioned writers view a network of kinfolk as crucial to an individual's well-being. But what about the dysfunctional aspects of the kindship network or its culture? Still, is there a value in knowing your family history? Alex Haley surmised that "in all of us there is a hunger, marrow deep, to know our heritage—to know who we are and where we came from. Without this enriching knowledge, there is a hollow yearning. No matter what our attainments in life, there is still a vacuum, an emptiness, and the most disquieting loneliness."[9] If such deep existential longing exists, as Haley claims, to know our heritage, perhaps family stories of feats and failures that are sheathed in life affirming values can be an identity marker, a source of inspiration, resilience, role modeling, and legacy building, as well as the sinew that binds families. Corey postulated that it is important to know family history: "For the younger generations, mostly, so that the kids can carry on the legacy, [especially since] things will change from generation to generation." People forget too easily to share their history.

As an entrepreneur, I was interested if Candace was influenced by the entrepreneurial spirit of her grandparents. She reflected for a moment and responded this way:

My mom, my daddy, and I moved to Atlanta when I was three months old, and I was not raised around the extended family. As I have learned more about my grandparents, maybe that is where I got it from. I heard how my grandmother would find all these things at the antique shop. I can remember hearing my aunts and uncles would go with her. My grandmother had a lot of entrepreneurial interests, but I did not make that connection until I was older. Now I appreciate a lot more what they have done. I appreciate the support from the entire family. This helps me to stay motivated, knowing my family was interested in being entrepreneurs. Usually, we get together at Thanksgiving, so I am learning more and more from my uncles and aunts. And as I hear more stories, I connect them to the influence on me. Obviously, Uncle Roscoe has gotten most of his past entrepreneurial skills from my grandparents. My grandfather built our family's home and he made a living in the [construction industry]. And that is a dream for me to create generational wealth for my family through entrepreneurship. The fact that they were able to sustain a family of twelve kids is very impressive, admirable, and honorable.

Whatever the entrepreneurial, financial, spiritual, social, mental, or physical struggles waged on the home front and the larger community by Pennie and Roscoe, the grandchildren are their link to binding their good name through the generational chain. For the Jameses, great value exists in knowing their family history. Corey stated it best when he wrote, "Everyone wants to belong somewhere. Everyone wants somewhere to call home. A place, no matter what happens, they can go and cry, laugh, love, and be loved. Knowing where you come from fuels the person you are today, and gives you the fuel to be the person you want to be." With that said, whispering of the generational link between Roscoe Sr. and his grandson Corey is best captured in Linda Goetsch's humble poem:

Remember me in the family tree
My name, my days, my strife;
Then I'll ride upon the wings of time
And live an endless life.

# CHAPTER SEVEN
## The Fruit of Pennie and Roscoe
## James's Good Name

Since "a tree is known by the fruit it bears," what kind of fruit is borne from Pennie and Roscoe James's family tree? To know, shake the tree and watch the welcoming branches dance in the spiritual winds. See that its boughs and twigs, nourished by the taproot of a value system that runs deep in the soil of their descendants' souls, wave and overflow with the low-hanging fruit of solidarity. It is an easy pick, arguably the most flavorful, peak-harvested outcome of their value system. But so is the value-added fruit of the entrepreneurial and communitarian spirit. The former is characterized by an individual ethos, while the latter is regarded as a collective code. For the latter fruit of the spirit, noble character is one of its many traits. Hence, it is little wonder why Pennie and Roscoe heeded the biblical warning "You reap what you sow" when they blended and synchronized the two. Afterward, they seeded and cultivated the minds of their offspring with both. Along with nurturing seeds of solidarity, their family tree harvested a cornucopia of entrepreneurs and servant leaders. The first is infused with the spirit of entrepreneurship and innovation, while the second is imbued with the spirit of service and an ethic of care. When the two are fused, they produce socially conscious entrepreneurs poised to create wealth and intergenerational mobility.

The typology in figure 7.1 represents the outcome of the core value system imparted by Pennie and Roscoe.[1]

Pierre Bourdieu reminds us that families create economic, symbolic, social, and cultural capital.[2] In both his personal life and in his business, the good name of Roscoe Sr. represents symbolic capital, while social capital embodies the solidarity of the Jameses' network and their collective business experience. Cultural capital is the family's accumulative knowledge and skills that increase the chances of social mobility in a stratified society. For the various forms of capital, the family stands as an essential building block and breeding ground for their transmission. Take, for example, the Jameses' familial value system of empowerment that incorporates the entrepreneurial spirit. It is an important form of cultural capital conveyed through the process of socialization within the family, not only by what Pennie and Roscoe said but what they did, how they codified and explained the reason for holding this value, and

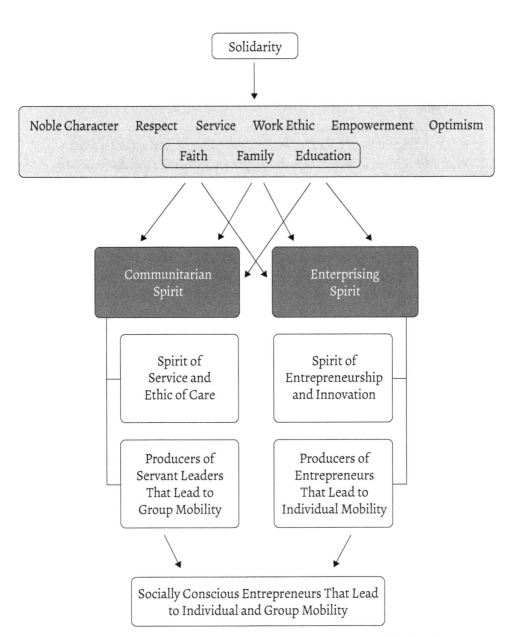

FIGURE 7.1 Model of leadership type, values, and worldview. Created by the author.

others like solidarity and service. Bourdieu also explicitly signals how cultural capital that is socialized within the family influences the development of particular styles, modes of representation, confidence, and the level of accumulated self-assurance in its members. He calls this process the "transmission of economic heritage."[3] That heritage is what Pennie and Roscoe successfully incubated and transmitted to their children. In doing so, they demonstrated the moxie and ingenuity of bootstrap entrepreneurship, while promoting solidarity and the spirit of service. Moreover, they managed to raise socially conscious entrepreneurs who have the intestinal fortitude to generate social, cultural, and economic capital for succeeding generations.[4]

Pennie and Roscoe painted guideposts for cultivating socially conscious entrepreneurs and innovators. Samuel, Wayne, Terri, Roscoe Jr., Shirley, Eric, and granddaughter Candace are examples of offshoots sprouting from the rootstock of their entrepreneurial tree. Since this spirit is not assured of being passed down to family members, how can the Jameses continue to maintain the intergenerational continuity of this ethos? Is storytelling one effective mechanism? Robert Smith believes storytelling is an essential device for transmitting family lore and a family culture of entrepreneurship. In the *New England Journal of Entrepreneurship*, he explores the role of storytelling in promoting familial entrepreneurship, but first he forewarns,

> Family businesses do not perpetuate themselves. Entrepreneurs must nurture and propagate the values that led to the creation of the very thing most precious to them—their business. This of course depends upon stability. Nor do these cherished values propagate themselves. To be made meaningful for others, and for future generations, family experiences, values and achievements must be communicated to others via language, narrative and storytelling or other forms embedded in narrative such as symbols. Often a variety of different socially constructed stories may be necessary contingent upon the situation, purpose, or need.[5]

Since storytelling is an important means for communicating the value of entrepreneurship, the narratives of Roscoe, Shirley, and Eric offer an intimate portrayal of their personal journeys to becoming entrepreneurs. Here, they share their hardscrabble realities of struggles and failures that came before the glory and their value system and support networks that sustained and nurtured them through difficulties. From adversity and success, they learned meaningful life lessons and developed critical business knowledge and skills to pass on to aspiring entrepreneurs. These lessons of feats and failures can be retold through generations.

The ensuing three narratives not only illustrate the business acumen of Pennie and Roscoe's offspring but also highlight their service orientation. As socially responsible entrepreneurs, their desire for profit is tempered with their passion to serve others, especially as Roscoe Sr. taught his children to always do "for the least of these." In our first story, we see how Roscoe Jr. creates economic opportunity for the poor and marginalized by hiring them for jobs and by providing on-the-job training. In the second story, through in-depth counseling, Shirley helps women to discover their value and purpose in life so they can reach their full potential. In the final story, through Touch A Life Academy, we see how Eric applies his skills and experiences as an educator to create a pedagogy of empathy for underserved youth in culturally diverse educational venues.

## I Am My Father's Son

*Roscoe James Jr.*

Before I begin my story, I want to share this poem my younger brother Wayne composed for me to show his appreciation, love, and support. I am so blessed and thankful to have his love and the love of all my family.

> I think about my Big Brother!
> When I think of my big brother, my thoughts put a smile on my face,
> When I think of my big brother, my thoughts remind me of God's grace!
> When I think of my big brother, my thoughts are flooded with music,
> When I think of my big brother, my thoughts are seeing him driving that '69 Buick,
> When I think of my big brother, my thoughts are of a hardworking man,
> When I think of my big brother, my thoughts are observing him with his drywall pan.
> Lastly, when I think of my big brother, my thoughts are about him helping others without a price,
> When I think of my big brother, my thoughts are "My big brother really loves Jesus Christ!"

Having my father's namesake, I always wanted to be just like him, a hardworking businessman, who was kind, loving, faithful, honest, and a generous man of his word. As his oldest son, I, along with my younger brothers Sam and Wayne, worked in his business, where he taught us from a very young age the craft of drywalling and plastering. I was expected to follow in my father's footsteps. But I took a detour.

Eventually, I retraced his footprints, and I did an about-turn in 1991 when I took over my father's business as his health began to wane from the ravages of Parkinson's disease. I successfully expanded the company, adding carpentry and other trades. Like my father, I, too, travel from Florida to Maine to work on contractual projects. And without a doubt, somewhere from above, I can hear him proclaim, I am today continuing his good name. I am now walking in his well-known footsteps, although missteps happened along the way, leaving footprints of sorrow and regret.

Perhaps, in some way, suffice it to say my life has been like a work of art. That is, when individuals see an exquisitely framed painting on a wooden canvas, they see only its frontside. They do not know what is on the backside of that picture, especially if the rear is messy. Rocks, dirt, and termites may be eating away at its back. In similar fashion, the complete picture of my life is also an eye-catching facade, but its backside has grime and gunk. I have certainly struggled with letting people know about that other side. However, at this point in my life, if you turn the picture over, people can see what God has done. I prayed to the Lord, beseeching, "How can I let people know about that murky side?" Then God reminded me of the ten lepers who got healed. One went back and gave God the glory. Then God asked him, "Where are the other nine? I delivered ten lepers." Not wanting to be remiss like the nine lepers, I needed to show gratitude for what God has done for me. I cannot hold back because I would do God an injustice if I did not touch down in deep waters of my life and let people know. So I decided to write my story.

My sorrowful and regretful, drama-filled life during young adulthood did not play out in a movie or television script. Instead, it played out in court starting in 1983. In one of those court appearances, here I stood as the one and only child of my parents' twelve children who had ever been in trouble with the law. Here I stood simmering in shame before my faithful, God-fearing, respectable, and loving family—my mom, dad, sisters, and brothers—who stood as paragons of virtue in the community and the idyllic family like *Little House on the Prairie*. Here I stood in front of a judge, awaiting my fate and feeling like a social leper, when he said, "Mr. James, you cannot drive any more until you get your license back." I had recently purchased a new car, and I was caught driving 15 mph over the speed limit, which was considered reckless driving in North Carolina. Entrenched in my youthful rebellion, I said, "They are not going to tell me how fast I should drive." My license was suspended when I was caught once again while driving. Appearing before the same judge, he remarked, "Mr. James, if you come in here one more time, you are going to jail and serve some time. You come from a great family. I know your dad." When he repeated that, it went in one ear and came out the other.

My "I don't care" attitude was on full display throughout this time of my youthful rebellion. Deep-seated anger gripped me. It stemmed from my father's acceptance of our family church's religious restrictions. During my eleventh-grade year, I was prohibited from participating in band camp like my friend Anthony. Throughout my high school years, I played the trombone, and I wanted to further my study in this area because I had an interest in becoming a professional musician. Anthony and I played together in the musical groups at our church, and he encouraged me to attend band camp so I could improve my skills and perhaps earn a music scholarship to college as he had. Even though I could not attend band camp at Northeastern High School or follow in his musical path, my friend continued to motivate and support me. In addition to being upset about band camp, prior to and after my graduation from high school, I was enraged by working for my father whom I remained dependent on for an income level. I continued working for Dad's business even after attending one semester of junior college at the College of Albemarle during my recovery from an on-the-job injury, where a roof beam collapsed on my leg, seriously injuring it. Dad miraculously lifted the roof from my trapped body and saved my leg. My dad loved me and I knew that he was trying to make ends meet to support the family. But I was angry for working so hard and not making enough money. I wanted to have a new bicycle, I wanted to dress in the latest fashion, and I wanted to have sufficient money in my pocket to spend like my friends. I was mad with the world because I could not have any of these things.

As a result of my anger and "I don't care" attitude, I was stopped again while driving on a suspended license. I faced the same judge again. This time, he quipped, "Mr. James, you have ten days." I responded, "Huh?" He repeated, "You have ten days." At that time, ten days in jail equated to three days, which meant you served a third of your time. For the entire three days I was in jail, I was confined there with high school classmates and a cousin. So for three days and nights, we spent jesting and joking with one another. It is what inmates call a happy pit stop.

After being released from jail, my "I don't care" attitude continued to prevail. When the judge stated, "Mr. James, you cannot drive for six months," I thought to myself, "I am going to move to Virginia. And by the way, since

I am going to be away from my mom, dad, sisters, and brothers, I am going to literally rev up the engine." During my defiant period, I had internal battles with myself. One way to escape from my angry self was to fill my life with material goods, so I purchased nice cars and a fashionable wardrobe. When I visited my brother Wayne at East Carolina University in 1986, I recalled how proud he felt about his big brother. How he had looked up to me as he introduced his peers! They gathered around my car and admired my clothes. They viewed me as a role model. But when I left campus that day in 1986, I felt like an imposter. I wanted to make a change. I was keenly aware that my parents had an excellent batting average of eleven home runs in raising children who had excellent grades in school. And I was the only one who struck out. I had bad grades. Often, it is the one that strikes out all the time and the one with the bad grades that parents should pay attention to most. But no one seems to understand the one who is struggling since he is a failure. He is the black ball of the family. He is a loser. Etched in my memory is a phrase my mom repeated to my dad in 1977, the year after graduating from high school in 1976: "Junior will never amount to anything." Given the route I was traveling and my unwavering brashness of "I don't care" attitude, I understand exactly what she meant. Those words stayed with me for a long time. Those words stayed in my ears: "You will never amount to anything." Those words stayed with me, but I also challenged them. I also remember my dad asking my siblings, "Do you all think Junior is on drugs or something?" "No! That's not Junior's thing," they echoed. True, drugs were never my thing, and I never used them. But I was, indeed, rebellious and an angry young man. Often, individuals want to avoid confronting their past. I do not like to remember myself this way, so I can understand the reason for avoidance.

Despite my delinquent behavior, I still maintained the love, concern, and support of my family. I would say to anyone, especially now as I look at my younger self, that if you ever get on a roll of not caring, you are headed for a fall. That fall came one day after numerous times of being caught speeding and driving on a suspended license. I was stopped for the same offense once again. Additionally, I was cited for purchasing stolen equipment, of which I was well aware, but I did not care that it was stolen. At the trial, the judge said, "Look, you got six months." I walked into the jail in Chesapeake, Virginia, thinking of all the traffic violations committed in North Carolina, Virginia, and even Maryland and sensing this time it would not be a fraternal happy pit stop with my cousin and high school classmates. I was alone in my darkness. They certainly did a scare aware on me when the jail door slammed with a clang behind me at the facility. Suddenly, I was caged like an animal for four months. After I was released, I volunteered to turn myself in for a traffic infraction committed in Maryland. When I arrived at the gate, the woman correctional officer asked why I was there. She was surprised when I told her I had come to turn myself in for the traffic violation and to get right with God. Even though I had irregularly paid off my fine, when I went before the judge, he remembered me and detained me.

During my various confinements, I was sent to six prisons. I spent five days at one prison, six days at a second one, and three days at still another prison. Then I was sent to Hagerstown, Maryland, for four months and then served time in Salisbury and Snow Hill, Maryland, for two months. Later, I was reclassified and sent to Baltimore, Maryland, for two months, where I worked in the kitchen until I was sent back to Salisbury.

In confinement, my struggles felt like I was living under a dark bridge. Being rebellious, I still did not want to listen to anyone, even with the haunting words of my thirteen-year-old baby brother's voice still ringing in my head as I made a collect call home from the correctional facility. Eric inquired, "Junior, where are you, and when are you coming home? I miss you." I replied, "I am locked up in Maryland." Eric asked, "Why? When are you going to get it right and make a change? I need you!" Silence gripped me. I had let my baby brother down. I had let my dad, mom, brothers, and sisters down. I grew angrier with myself, with others, with the world, and with God.

But here in my darkest hour, God met me on August 25, 1987, and on an 83-degree day, I was saved. I never liked sharing this part of my life story. But when God came to me, I said, "Lord, I cannot let anyone know my struggles." I will never forget what God whispered in my ear with a small still voice: "I have seen it. Who are they?" Then God threw me a morsel of thought from Apostle Paul to chew. In writing to believers in Philippi, he said, "But one thing I do: forgetting what lies behind and straining forward to what lies ahead, I press on toward the goal for the prize of the upward call of God in Jesus Christ." The Apostle Paul had lived a life he had come to regret before his encounter with Jesus on the road to Damascus. He persecuted and killed Christians. But he was healed from his spiritual blindness and given a new name and a new mission. Although he was imprisoned and still had his burdens, I believe the same God that spoke to Paul spoke to me in that little voice that hot summer day in 1987.

With God's love washing over me and transforming me, here is where I buried that old Roscoe James Jr. I was twenty-nine years old. God did this to me and for me at the darkest moments of my life to help others. So I affirmed to the Lord, "I am not going to wait until I get out of jail; my ministry starts here." I consider this occurrence of listening to God's will to be His servant while imprisoned as one of the greatest events in my life. I am blessed my father and mother could witness that day. Only God brought me from dark times to where I am today, as I held fast to biblical Scriptures of my family's upbringing to draw comfort while imprisoned. One Scripture contended that when a righteous man falls seven times, he rises again. Along with my faith and the consistent love, care, and prayers of my family, I kept rising.

From that hour I met God on August 25, 1987, in the Chesapeake, Virginia, correctional facility, it did not matter thereafter to what facility I was sent because God found favor for me to encourage and build the morale of inmates.[6] I was fortunate that the young men also found favor in me. They would say, "This guy is pastoring, and he is locked up." I assured them, "I am locked up, but I am not locked out. And one of the greatest things God designed was confinement." Earlier in my ministry, one inmate asked me to pray with him because he was breaking up with his wife. When I made inroads into the church prison ministry groups who visited the facility, I was able to talk with more inmates. Since I was already steeped in a strong religious grounding, it was easy for me to make a solid connection with these groups as I spent much time with them. As I became close to them, I started playing the piano and reading the Scripture to them as well as talking to the inmates. Then church groups would say, "Yes, we could use this guy right in here." So when the church groups were not visiting, I delivered the sermons to the inmates until the church groups returned. When it was time to have service, the participants would say, "Pastor Roscoe, it's your night."

Very early during my confinement, other inmates thought I was an undercover cop because of the fast moves I was making. I was allowed by the officers to speak with different groups in prison because I had earned their trust. Once while I was in detention at Salisbury, Maryland, a riot broke out. Since the facility had some good officers there, two of them said, "Go get Roscoe to talk to these guys." These officers could have been more aggressive with the protesters. But instead, they said, "No, go get Roscoe! He can talk to them and pull off something." The guys had stuffed paper towel tissues down the toilets to flood the floors. The water did back up. I asked the officers to "give me a bucket and a mop." Then I stated, "I am going down there with them, and we are going to get this up." When I arrived there, I said, "Look, guys, I'm with you all." I remained at the site until we removed all the water. It was teamwork, so we had to stay together. Not only did I help the inmates, once a correctional officer who was having marital problems with his wife asked me to pray for him and his family.

God used me to do His work, no matter the correctional facility. When I returned to Salisbury, Maryland, I was placed on their work release program. During leisure time when we played basketball, football, baseball, or horseshoes, I would stop the play and reach for my Bible. Then we would find some guys to study the Scriptures. Afterward, we would proceed to the music room and sing songs like "At the Cross" that mostly everyone was familiar. They heard these songs while growing up, so it was not necessary to rehearse them. We also had a testimonial service for anyone who wanted to give praise to God and for anyone having problems at home. We wanted to connect these guys with their families. God was using me so mightily that He gets all the glory. Many nights I would cry, though not from being sad but from tears of joy. The other inmates would say, "Pastor Roscoe, come over to the K Block cell because some guy is going through tough stuff at home with his wife or children, and I want you to pray for him." I would say, "If I can do it, you can do it."

In the secure unit, I reached across the aisle to many individuals, so when I left the correctional facility in Salisbury, Maryland, the inmates hated to see me go. They cried like a baby. When you see how God uses His might against His apostles, you know God can still use you. Basically, I was locked up doing God's work. We can be a prisoner without being in jail. Many of us are locked up in our minds. I know this to be true because as I unlocked my mind, God used me to show my fellow prisoners how to unlock their minds by sharing with them the blessings of using whatever talents they possess despite their station in life. My mind was also open to receiving God's blessings and to being faithful to Him when I was hired as a day laborer in the release program of a marble and drywall company in Salisbury. It was as though God spoke to me, saying, "Be faithful with a few things, and I will make you ruler over many." I was a faithful worker, and I succeeded beyond my wildest imaginings. In the four months that I worked for the company, I went from $1 daily to $3 daily to $620 weekly. After four months, I had accumulated $13,000 because I worked above and beyond the time required in the work release program. I worked at rest stops along Highway 13 a month or so before the release program began. Each Friday, we had to release our pay checks to the pickup driver who transported us daily to work. If I worked longer hours, someone from the company would return me to the correctional facility. I will never forget when Mr. Armstrong, the first officer at the facility, said, "You are locked up, so how in the world are you making more money than me?" I also worked at Salisbury State College. The owner must have liked my work ethic because he asked, "Will you promise to come back and work with us when you get out?" I said, "I sure will." I was still locked up, so I was giving thanks to God. Once I was released, they said, "He is not coming back." But when I showed up, they were shocked. I said, "What you did for me, I can do all what God led me to do!" When I left the company, I returned to Virginia as a changed man.

Christmas Eve, December 24, 1990, this changed man returned home to see family. And I am forever grateful for God's love and His power. One of the greatest things outside of God's Holy Spirit is God's Word. It offered peace of mind during my dimmest days of imprisonment. Without God and the supporting cast of my family—parents, brothers, and sisters—I could not have done this alone. My family was behind me, like some horses, pushing me along. They said, "Junior is not going down like this!" I made them angry, but my family did not give up on me. I love the heck out of every last one of them. God did too much for me to hold my mouth from praising Him and my family. I must continue to show gratitude like the one leper in the biblical Scripture. To see God move, reshape, and form me into the man He wants me to be, I must switch hands and get right with God. In my need to switch hands, I am forced to think of my three brothers who acted like big brothers and protectors while I was incarcerated. Oh, my God! Sam stuck by me. Wayne stuck by me. Indeed, they were my big brothers and I am proud of all three. I really do not have the words to describe those three guys. It was unbelievable to see how they maintained the upkeep of the house while I was away. Thankfully, through the power of God and the prayers of my parents and my eleven siblings, I have stayed with the promises that I made to the Lord.

In addition to my parents and siblings, my wife, Machell, stood by me through all the drama. Clearly, I can understand her reason for standing by my side now that I turned my life around, but she stood by me when I did not have a penny in my pocket. At the time of my incarceration, we were not married. However, she waited for me and supported me during my journey of confinement. I remember thinking one day to myself, "I do not know when I am coming home. How unfair is it to keep her at bay this way?" At that moment, I almost picked up the phone to call and tell her, "Go ahead with your life. I do not want to be accountable for your waiting for me because I might get out of here and go crazy." By the time I was ready to dial the phone, I had changed my mind. She waited for me until I came home, and we have been married for twenty-nine years. One of our favorite songs that we sing together is "There Must Be a God Somewhere." It symbolizes our journey of struggle and hope. Sometimes we think that whatever we are going through, God is not there. But He is right there with us.

I am grateful that God was with me, like He was with the Prodigal Son who returned home to a loving and forgiving father. All I ever wanted was to be like my dad. And I never blue-penciled that part of being like him out of life's movie, even though I was the only one of his twelve children to stray from the biblical path of training up a child in the way he should go, and he will not depart from it. I had hurt and embarrassed my parents. I became so rebellious that I started to do wrong in life. But seemingly, God had other plans for me. Interestingly, before leaving prison, Mom, Debbie, and Sam visited me. When Sam asked, "What are your plans?" I responded, "I am going to take over Dad's business." Pleading for God's mercy, I asked Him to give me the strength, the power, the will, and the way to help my dad with his business as his health began to decline. Oh, my Lord! When my dad learned that I took over his business, he expressed the most joy I have ever seen, especially when he saw one of my custom ceiling designs. Since I was a little boy, I watched him create his swirled ceilings. As Dad was lying on his deathbed, I took his hand and held it, then I said, "I got it now." I would take care of the business he built. My brother Sam was also pleased as well as supportive when I took over our dad's business. Although he had recently started his career at NASA, in his spare time, he helped with the business when I initially took charge. One day, we were renovating the studio of an R & B star in Virginia Beach. I asked one of the producers if I could play the keyboard. He gave me a questioning look like, "You can play?" After I played, Sam said, "Roscoe, when you jumped on that piano, the sound filled the room with glee, and it was one of my proudest moments of you." The sound of Sam's support was like music to my ears, knowing that I struck some low notes in life, but I was rising and hitting high notes as the Scripture predicted.

At last, I am hitting the high notes in my business, which is located in Virginia Beach and serves primarily the Hampton Roads area as prophesied. Like my father, I travel from Florida to Maine for business ventures. And I also work across the aisle with the powerful and less powerful. On the one hand, I have established excellent relationships with Lowe's and Home Depot. They have extended the courtesy of allowing me to park my company trucks and work equipment in their parking lots. On the other hand, my employees are hirees from Union Mission, Salvation Army, and juvenile detentions. I have helped some of them to start their own business. I believe in reaching across the aisle to help those who are struggling in life. Dark clouds and deep struggles are the major entities that brought me to where I am today, and they continue as my supporting beams. Therefore, when something has changed you, when you have been in contact with God's spirit, you are never the same. So I have made it my platform to help steer, motivate, and instill God's power in young men who have been locked out of societal opportunities or locked up in prison. In fact, I work with people from all walks of life who have been through some tough challenges. Not everybody who has been to prison is a bad person. As I stated previously, some people have never been locked up, but they are still stuck in their minds. They also still need someone to love them. I have done work for people with million-dollar homes to ten-million-dollar homes, and they, too, confide in me about having children who are using drugs, getting locked up, stealing their money, and sneaking out of the home at night. The local television reporters do not frequent these expensive areas, and often, that is where your major struggles are, though never televised. Instead, they go to areas that are disproportionately saturated with low-income housing like the projects. I know because these families open up and talk with me one-on-one and ask, "What can I do?" I think, "What can I say to them?" If your spirit is involved and your occupation is out of it, the spirit is doing the work. According to Apostle Paul, it is the work of the spirit that is using me. I do believe God uses His work and His service through me like the lady on the front porch waiting for the mailman to come. It is not the mailman; it is that check he is bringing in that package.

Today, when people look at me, they only see the righteous Roscoe, a successful businessman and minister of God's Word. They do not see the rebellious Roscoe, who spent time incarcerated, so they always put me on a pedestal. I say to them, "Don't judge the book by its cover" because they don't know what's in the middle. They like the beginning of the book and its ending, but the middle is what most cannot handle. They don't like the part where the mother and father are fighting. But that's the part where the healing comes.

And the healing has come in telling my story as the only one of twelve children who has ever had brushes with the law. I never liked talking about it because I embarrassed my family. My principal hurdle was getting over what people would think. Truly, it was my toughest song. But God got me over it when He spoke to me, saying, "I delivered you like the three Hebrew boys." Finally, I arrived at the point where I had to get this out of me. I said, "Lord, I cannot hold this anymore. If I keep this to myself, what is the purpose of being delivered?" I realized that sharing my story could help touch and motivate somebody else.

In 2010, I began to really drop the veil by letting people know that the way that I am viewed today has not always been that way. As I started having deeper conversations with people about what I had been through, here are some of their reactions: "You came from a religious family, and you were always in church. Your sisters couldn't wear pants and everywhere they went, they had to wear dresses. Your family was known as a church family, and your family was the *Little House on the Prairie*." Others exclaimed, "Not you, Roscoe!" I would say, "Yes, what you see is what God has done." When I was told, "That's the past," I would say, "Look, you do not know who may be struggling out there. Many people with money are struggling with hurts and pain, and they try to fill it with money or the wrong stuff. I had to fill my hole with Jesus."

It is my belief that it was part of God's plan to navigate me through all my struggles. With that said, I would not exchange my struggles for anything in the world because of my greater understanding of myself. God can use individuals like me to help others admit there is a way out. I messed up, but now I have turned my life around and I am blessed up. I have a saying on my Facebook page, "If I can do it, you can do it."

## Self-Discovery with Shirley

*Shirley Dickerson*

When I awake at dawn, I start with this daily prayer: "Father, thank You for making Your home in my heart. I need Your presence today, Lord. Help me to honor You with my thoughts and words and to be a blessing to those around me. Amen."

I believe when we walk in faith, hope, and love, it gives us the power to accept and own our truth, which can lead to breakthroughs in overcoming psychological barriers of guilt, pain, shame, and trauma that block healing and wholeness. But as Marianne Williamson noted, "It takes courage . . . to endure the sharp pains of self-discovery rather than choose to take the dull pain of unconsciousness that would last the rest of our lives." Through my own gut-wrenching, soul-searching journey, I know that Williamson's assertion rings true. For today, I am consciously walking that courageous path of self-reflection, healing, and wholeness, and I want to assist in empowering others in their journey toward a more mindful and purpose-driven life. It is my reason for starting a service-oriented business, Self-Discovery with Shirley, in January 2020. The impetus for my business grew out of a life-changing involvement with the ministries of Shannon Evette, my mentor and spiritual teacher, who founded the Worthy Healing Academy and the Sanctuary Global in Los Angeles, California, where I became certified in the Worthy Method Life Coach program in 2019.

It is the mission of my practice to guide clients in making intentional life choices about what they need to create, preserve, eliminate, and accept in their interpersonal relationships, professional relationships, and more important, relationship with self. Too often, we are captives of our past because we carry old negative mental tapes in our heads. I firmly believe we can replace these old tapes and transcend our personal limitations, our self-sufferings, and our fear-based habits of procrastination and self-doubt. I believe our fears compromise the beauty and revelations of God's will. Each time we expand our hearts to love ourselves and each other, we destroy the "enemy of fear." When we destroy the foe of fear, shame, and guilt, it activates our blessings and our truth and love. The Scripture Jeremiah 29:11 tells us, "For I know the plans I have for you, declares the LORD, plans to prosper you and not to harm you, plans to give you hope and a future."

By taking an audit of adverse emotions and beliefs, clients can begin the process of supplanting them with love, joy, patience, kindness, understanding, hope, faith, gentleness, and peace. Having a clear and focused awareness of negative emotions can help them begin the process of decluttering the mind by evaluating underlying assumptions and interpretations, a necessary step before considering alternative possibilities. Only then can clients begin to align their mental, spiritual, and physical health to achieve freedom, clarity, purpose, and a sense of well-being. Ultimately, it is my goal to guide clients to accept and believe they are worthy of wholeness and healing through the rituals of self-love and self-care practices, which include encouraging individual clients to develop intimate devotional practices and honoring themselves and God. Each day, clients are encouraged to carve out some uninterrupted time, preferably in the morning, to practice spoken self-affirmative mantras or to practice journaling, reading, or doing soul work to create healthier habits and to also work toward shifting unbelief to belief, faith, courage, confidence, and improved self-esteem.

As a certified life coach, my practice is grounded in a biblical framework, and in that vein, my vision is to create a safe space to express unsafe feelings as well as to create a place where individuals of diverse beliefs can transcend the hidden perils of unresolved psychic scars that preclude them from reaching their full potential. To create an emotional safe space, first and foremost, it is essential to establish an open, hospitable, and caring atmosphere conducive to sharing feelings, thoughts, and beliefs. Second, creating an emotional safe space for individuals requires nonjudgmental listening and understanding to facilitate clients in overcoming inner fears and inhibitions. Third, creating an emotional safe space also implies being culturally sensitive. It is therefore important to acknowledge and understand the contextual background of clients along gender, ethnicity, race, class, and age as a way to facilitate well-being, build courage and confidence, and to make lucid life choices so clients can become their best selves. Finally, creating an emotional safe space means allowing your clients sufficient time to honestly explore negative inner thoughts and feelings. Often, we tend to talk from our wounded places instead of our worthy places. Providing adequate time gives clients a greater opportunity to process alternative ways of thinking and coping that are more likely to lead to positive outcomes. Having a clear framework regarding an emotional safe space enables me to more effectively guide clients to accept and believe they are worthy of wholeness and healing when an atmosphere of trust prevails. This perspective sets my practice apart from others. Viewing an emotional safe space in this way is advantageous to clients I serve, including men, because it is more inclusive. It is also most suitable for my largely female, multigenerational, and international clients who are seeking to find a voice of hope over despair.

Shauna L. Hoey, in *Fire of Hope*, believes "our brokenness summons light into the deepest crevices in our hearts." Light has always been in my heart, but at times so has brokenness, and here is where I enter with my story and how it precipitated my business. My light has always been my family and my faith. I am fortunate to have grown up in a very loving, close-knit, honorable, and faithful family who served and worshipped God unwaveringly. My parents made enormous emotional and social investment in their twelve children, which contributed to an enriching life experience and a source of social and spiritual wealth. As an adult, I have come to recognize and appreciate their tremendous sacrifice. Because of the influence of my family, I developed a heart to serve people and a desire to show the active love of God through compassion, authenticity, honesty, trust, love, kindness, patience, restoration, understanding, consistency, and joy—the fruits of the spirit. I also developed deep crevices in my heart where no light had shone, even though I experienced love and joy within my family. I also felt some sense of brokenness while growing up as a young Christian girl.

I ranked seventh in birth order of twelve children within my family. As a middle child, I remember having a gentle and quiet spirit, sometimes so placid and silent that my voice was unheard. I was like the dove in Song of Solomon 2:14, hiding in the "clefts of the rock, in the crannies of the cliff," until I grew accustomed to not using my voice to pursue my aspirations or my talents, although I had a passion to do more and be more. I loved art, and I had the ability to sketch well. I was also quite good in sports, excelling in softball, volleyball, tennis, basketball, as well as sprinting. However, my God-fearing family belonged to a religious organization that subscribed to a doctrine that, in my opinion, limited my growth capacity and my courage to use my voice to explore my talents and creativity. I remember one of the doctrinal tenets of my childhood church did not favor women actively serving in leadership roles the same way as men in church. Another doctrinal tenet had a restrictive dress code. We had to conform to rules regarding what we could or could not wear. This was particularly the case for me and the older siblings, especially my sisters during our coming of age. As young women, our religion was not as supportive of opportunities to dream big and explore the world with our singing and acting talents, nor was it supportive of pursuing professional sports. So I was beset by feelings of doubt and unworthiness that reinforced some self-limiting beliefs. These misgivings continued well into my adulthood and inhibited me from rising to my fullest potential. Sometimes we do not manifest God's order regarding ourselves, our love relations, our finances, our professions, our education, and our businesses. Still, I always knew in my heart that God wanted to elevate my sense of self-worth, self-love, and self-confidence and use and expand my gifts and talents.

I felt this deeply after surviving my first marriage. After seventeen years of being in what I considered a good marriage, I was surprised when it ended in 2005. We had three beautiful, intelligent, graceful daughters who are now successful young women in their own rights. The divorce was devastating. Despite the ups and downs of married life, I always held true to my marital vow until death do us part, even when our matrimonial hems began fraying around our value differences in religion and child-rearing. Shortly after I married my former husband, we moved to Atlanta, Georgia, and when the marriage ended, I was left to raise three daughters. I was fortunate because I had a good-paying job, but after six years with that company, I was laid off. I could not keep my home, and I also lost my automobile. I found myself homeless in the midst of the 2008 recession but not hopeless. I believed God would restore it all in my life.

To help me acknowledge and assess some of my major losses at that point, I joined a women's support group after my divorce. The group offered some solace, encouragement, support, and a safe space for evaluating and coming to terms with what had happened in our lives. It also offered an opportunity to vent deep anxieties, angers, and frustrations. Despite the benefits, too many of its members were mired in their big hurts and sufferings.

Although I was also hurting, at times, it seems after the sessions were over, I was the only one to find a silver lining in all the adversities despite being empathetic to what each person endured. For me, too much negativity without working toward a resolution manifests itself in a fatalistic world-view. I needed a life change. But first, I had to surrender to God, and I had to let go of old negative self-assumptions and feelings of doubt, shame, embarrassment, guilt, and unworthiness. We want God's will to line up with our comfort zones. But sometimes a rebirth dictates undergoing some messiness, vulnerabilities, and truth telling if we expect to make meaning of our lives as we work to overcome traumas. So I began my self-discovery and empowerment journey of personal growth, purposeful activation, and spiritual awareness. Happily, at the core of my being, I always had a deep and abiding faith that God is strategically assigning people with great wisdom, knowledge, and discernment who have overcome traumas to make connection with spiritually wounded individuals. These wisdom-mongers help others make meaning out of their hurts to restore them to healing and wholeness.

When I entered my restoration season, I asked God how I can serve Him. The answer came when I joined a new church in 2012 and decided to become a group leader of ten to twelve women for one year. I thoroughly enjoyed my lay ministerial role working with these women. During this time, I also started a full-time position in a top-500 corporation, where I was soon promoted to a leadership role. At last, I felt God had given me a new lease on life, and I was beginning to feel anchored.

Besides asking God how I can serve Him during this restorative phase, I asked Him to send me a good husband because I wanted to remarry. Specifically, I asked God for a husband who would love me and who would also love God. I made a covenant with God. I would wait for Him to guide me, and I would take no action of my own by getting involved in the dating scene. Instead, I would allow God to send me my husband, a man of the spirit, and the husband God wanted me to have. After being divorced for ten years and after having experienced so much disappointment, my new man of God, now husband, lover, best friend, and soulmate, found me in the most unexpected place. It was at the coffee station in my new workplace, where I was making my new start. I had always vowed that I would never date anyone on my job. But sometimes, we must be open to God, so I embraced that notion. When my future husband asked me what I did in my free time, I told him I enjoyed being a small group leader for my church. He was so impressed with my devotion to God and my ministry that he asked for a date.

Our first date was a Sunday visit to his church. I felt God had given me a new lease on life by placing my feet on solid ground. We have been together for seven blessed years. And we have been happily wedded for four of them.

As I settled into my new life, I felt a calling to advocate and to carry a mantle of leadership for those who are oppressed and marginalized in spirit. It was not for fame or fortune but for honor as a servant leader. I wanted my story to become an impetus for overcoming obstacles. I feel if you have not lived an experience, you cannot teach it, so I chose to make room for something spoken to me from God. This Scripture from Isaiah 61:1–3 speaks to my calling: "The Spirit of the Sovereign LORD is on me, because the LORD has anointed me to proclaim good news to the poor. He has sent me to bind up the broken-hearted, to proclaim freedom for the captives and release from darkness for the prisoners, to proclaim the year of the LORD's favor and the day of spirit of despair. . . . They will be called oaks of righteousness, a planting of the LORD for the display of his splendor." As stated earlier, since childhood, I have always felt a deep compassion and empathy for others. I desire to pour my gift of compassion and empathy into spiritually and emotionally wounded clients whom I serve. Using my empathetic listening ear as a support, accountability, and validation partner, I want to share their journey toward breakthroughs and recoveries from addictions, abuse, bad relationships, economic suffering, and low self-esteem. I also want to help guide them to embrace their healing and transformation. However, I could not move forward to share their journey until I could tell and accept my story. To engage otherwise means my bestowed gifts would not be fully released. To seek a deeper truth and love, we must own our story and not allow it to own us.

In seeking that deeper truth, I can now face my strengths and limitations. Having greater clarity and purpose, it is now easier for me to respond proactively to my triggers and blind spots rather than reacting negatively to them. With greater courage, discipline, and purpose, I no longer become defensive about everything that conflicts with my opinions or beliefs. I can bounce back quicker when I do fail. I can dream again. And I do not feel that I am my mistakes. I am also not afraid to face my truths.

My spiritual calling and entrepreneurial spirit that I first learned at the knee of my parents, along with my other core personal values and behaviors, moved into alignment with my business vision and values in January 2020 when I launched my ministerial business. Only then, after accepting and owning my story, was I ready to accept the calling on my life by God to utilize my spiritual gifts. According to God's Word, I have always believed He has placed in my heart the notion we should be generous toward others and we should learn to forgive, let go of our offenses, and live in peace. When we choose to be intentional with our words and actions, while giving thanks to God and lifting others, we will feel connected to God all throughout our day. I feel that connection more than ever as my spiritual gifts operate in tandem with my core values of faith, discernment, generosity, love, and respect for self and others in my personal life. These values overlap with the following key eight core tenets of my business, which are derived from my mentor Shannon Evette's book *Worthy*:

*Key One. Courage*—when we can release the need to control the outcome and trust that we are living our way into the answers.

*Key Two. Choice*—how we design and cocreate our lives.

*Key Three. Connections*—relationships that expand our sense of value, expectations, self-respect, and self-love.

*Key Four. Compassion*—the ability to be kind, gentle, and understanding with yourself and others.

*Key Five. Clarity*—the ability to separate the fear-based thoughts from love-based wisdom.

*Key Six. Character*—develops by being consistent with your commitments.

*Key Seven. Called*—having a quiet knowing and understanding within that you were born for something unique and something more.

*Key Eight. Complete*—not lacking anything and not limited in any way.

I launched my business on New Year's Day 2020 with great enthusiasm and optimism. However, I faced challenges like all of us during the COVID-19 pandemic, the economic downturn, and the social unrest. After a slow business unveiling, I had to reevaluate my strategy while balancing expectations of my day job in corporate America, especially with all the adjustments occurring simultaneously. I began to feel some frustrations and doubts. During one of my routine morning walks, where I spend my intimate devotional time with God, I asked if He was really calling me to coach. If so, please send me a sign, message, or a God wink. That same day in June 2020, I received an unexpected call from a colleague with whom I worked but had no contact for over a year. She asked if I was still coaching and also queried me about the type of coaching [I did]. After I explained, she booked an appointment with me. She then offered a compliment, stating she looked up to me and admired my growth and personal success. The following month, I started teaching and coaching women all over the world through my affiliate organization, the Worthy Healing Academy.

My practice expanded rapidly, and now, not only do I have the honor of coaching women from the United States but also the United Kingdom, Australia, Jamaica, and Canada via online services. My counseling topics range from such issues as broken marriages and other personal relationships, job loss, ministerial calling, spiritual gifts, trauma, and self-worth and self-esteem concerns. If the women I initially advise at Worthy Healing Academy desire more in-depth coaching, they become my clients at Self-Discovery with Shirley. Emerging from my practice is the common theme of women not feeling worthy of God's abundance. It is my role to introduce biblical principles that reinforce how believing in their own value honors God. These biblical principles and Scriptures, also the source of my own values and inspiration, sustained my parents while raising their large family and sustained members of my family and myself during trials and triumphs. I believe the glory of God is upon us and is manifested in many of us during the pandemic. Scripture Joshua 1:9 says, "Have I not commanded you? Be strong and courageous. Do not be afraid; do not be discouraged, for the Lord your God will be with you wherever you go."

In passing my values on to the next generation, I have taught my three daughters, who are steeped in the Christian faith, to trust God and to believe in themselves. I have also taught them the importance of feeling worthy, valuable, whole, and healed while they are on their life journey. They have become successful young adults, and each has a passion to serve others. Candace, my oldest daughter, adopted the entrepreneurial skills and passions of her grandparents, uncles, and mother. As a computer science-technology entrepreneur, she is owner and CEO of Myavana, a successful digital, personalized hair care company. Jasmine, my middle daughter, graduated from college as a medical assistant major. She has worked several years as a medical assistant with a large internal medicine practice. She also works part time as a customer care representative for Myavana. My youngest daughter, Paige, a college graduate with a BS in public policy, works for a nonprofit organization that provides support services for the underserved.

I serve the larger community by passing on the optimistic values and spiritual legacies of Roscoe and Pennie James. I believe that we are operating in God's abundant season of grace, mercy, wisdom, kindness, gentleness, faithfulness, healing, favor, breakthroughs, and blessings. We are here on earth to fulfill God's divine mission and purpose for kingdom living. Our souls are ever-changing and cocreatively inviting challenges in our lives to help us purify our hearts and minds. Unworthiness, fear, and self-sabotage invite unhealthy and unnecessary suffering that negate our God-given talents and calling. When we take a stand and align with God's purpose for our lives, we become people of great faith and character. We also become visionaries and responsible beings.

When I assist others in becoming their best selves, I am also becoming the best friend, coach, partner, soulmate, lover, wife, mother, sister, and daughter that I can be to my family and community. Equally, I am constantly evolving into the disciplined, ethical, intuitive, and influential woman of God and life coach, a necessary requisite to effectively assist individuals in discovering and activating their purpose, growth, healing, wholeness, and true calling.

## Why I Became an Entrepreneur

*Eric James*

I was released from Virginia Beach City Public Schools as a student support specialist in 2018 for replying to a young schoolgirl's posting on Instagram. She wrote that she loved me for helping her with her alcohol problem. I responded by saying I loved her back, and I cared for her like she was my own daughter. When I think back to John Alan Lee's color wheel theory of love that I learned during my undergraduate years of college, it was agape love for me, the universal love of all humanity I learned at my parents' knee and in my Christian church. Judging from the human resources representative and his female assistant's glassy stares of revulsion, they desired to spin a tale of *ludus* love or playful love, falsely accusing me of inappropriate behavior with a young woman. I felt like I was being flung in the ashes of vengeance for serving my students. Yet it also freed me to assist them in nontraditional ways. Here was my opportunity to rise from the ashes like the phoenix, the mystical bird, and soar to new heights by opening my own academy to serve students in a way that was tailored to meet their individual needs. Now they could spread their wings and mount up from the vestiges of hopelessness and despair.

With that impetus, I founded Touch A Life Academy in 2018, a venture that provides youth outreach services. Its mission is to build an organization designed to improve, enrich, empower, and direct the life of a child. Presently, I am serving elementary, middle school, high school, and college students. I also collaborate with professionals in related fields who need additional support to assist students in improving their quality of life. It is my vision to reach youth globally with my message of hope and to help motivate them to succeed. Linking people and resources is central to fulfilling my mission and vision.

The year 2007 was pivotal for me. First, it led to a defining clarity in purpose, mission, and vision for my life. Second, I married my wife and kindred spirit, Malissa Gordon, and moved to Virginia Beach, Virginia, without a definitive job prospect. Having faith that God would provide meaningful employment, I felt fortunate to have found a job as a teacher's assistant with the Virginia Beach City Public Schools several months after my arrival in the city. Even though I was overqualified for the position, my success as a teacher's assistant opened the door to a position in my area of expertise. Later that year, I was hired as a student support specialist, a dream job in the same school system. I was tasked with the responsibility of motivating students from underresourced backgrounds to achieve academic excellence, to improve and monitor their school attendance, and to encourage prosocial behaviors in two highly diverse schools, a middle school and a high school. The demographic composition of the schools was largely middle-class whites, approximately 60 percent; the other 40 percent of the students were mostly minorities from poor and low-income backgrounds. In general, I worked with the latter population, which dovetailed with both my purpose and passion. I knew my purpose was to be a light unto the world, and that aspiration paralleled my passion to help inspire and influence the mental, emotional, behavioral, moral, and social lives of youth. I sensed this position was well suited for my temperament because I had mastered the art of patience while caring for my father during his illness. It also helped that I have a strong service orientation as well as a cache of moral values instilled by my parents, such as respect, faith, fair play, family togetherness, and love. Furthermore, as an HBCU graduate, I witnessed how the lives of students were positively impacted when nurturing and caring educators pushed students to achieve and guided their career aspirations and personal development. At North Carolina A&T State University, I found my passion after I was assisted by my college advisor. When the counselor administered a career assessment and personality test, it led to a change in major from computer science to child psychology. My work experiences have confirmed the importance of this test as well as validated my change of course in college. Working primarily in the field of human services also prepared me for the position of student support specialist.

Upon graduating from college, I took a position as a grocery manager in one of the local chain stores in Greensboro, North Carolina. I worked there in the evening; during the day, I directed an after-school program for the YMCA. Although I was successful as a store manager, I found the business world operated quite differently from the human services field. The bottom line for business is profit. The bottom line in the human services field is people and serving their personal and social needs. I left corporate America and entered the school system. At that time, I also returned to the YMCA to work with the after-school program. Later, I was encouraged to enter the mental health field, and I was hired at a behavioral health center, where I worked with adults, adolescents, and children. My role was to help clients overcome depression and hopelessness by identifying, honoring, and working with that component of their being. As the son of Roscoe James Sr., I knew how to inspire joy and hope and to listen without judging. "Do not judge, or you, too, will be judged." While working there, I encountered my first experience with suicidal patients. It was unsettling to me that death was actually an option to escape what they were enduring in this world. Even though suicide appeared to be a personal act, it led me to see that suicide was also a social act. I gained further insights into human behavior when I was hired at the county juvenile detention center in Greensboro, North Carolina. Through personal and group counseling, I wanted to offer another way of thinking about life to these troubled youths who lacked guidance, structure, and meaning in their lives in order to reduce the rate of reoffending. As a result of my effective counseling sessions with the juvenile population, the rate of reoffending improved, and I received a promotion. Still, one cannot be effective alone; teamwork is important. Not only did I learn teamwork in my home and while participating in the band in high school and in college, but it was also reinforced when I served as the director of restore operations for Habitat for Humanity. Teamwork is crucial to improving the lives of others.

With a variety of skill sets acquired in these prior positions, I was ready to take on the challenge of being the best in my new post as student support specialist. For me, this position was more than a nine-to-five job. I was fully engaged in pushing students to succeed and in using whatever tools, time, and techniques available. It was important to go beyond the call of duty and to find creative ways to connect with them. This occurred even while serving as a teacher's assistant. One day, I was on my way to the YMCA to exercise after school when I encountered three middle school boys who asked me to play basketball with them. Their request was unexpected, so for a moment, I had to imagine being in their position. I decided to play basketball that afternoon with them. The next time we played, ten students showed up, then fifteen, then twenty, and then thirty. Although these students enjoyed their recreational outlets of playing basketball, more important, I learned they needed a positive adult male role model who cared about their interests and who was also willing to spend time with them in an affirmative emotional climate. In sharing my time with these students, I surmised their sense of home was not a safe sanctuary. My heart was touched by this understanding, so I incorporated this insight into my position as student support specialist. I began to build positive relationships with students inside and outside of the classroom. It was important to remember and adhere to the biblical passage "The harvest is plenty, but the laborers are few." I chose to patiently labor long hours after school in the educational vineyard with underserved students, knowing that a life of toil was a gift bestowed on my heart. As a result of my approachability and my concern for students, I observed throughout the school day a common pattern. No matter the venue, hordes of students in both middle and high school sought me out for small talk, for counseling sessions, or just to greet me. It was one of the greatest feelings in the world because they felt safe and welcomed in my presence.

Although approximately 70 percent of my caseload fell into the poor or low-income category of being academically at risk and disproportionately minorities, I was extremely elated to mentor and support my students to see a brighter path for themselves. To care for the least of these is what I had always been taught by my father. Not only did I desire to improve their academic standing, but I also wanted to assist them in developing important life skills. I began to identify students who required not only guidance, support, mentoring, and leadership development but also students who needed a caring adult role model with an empathetic listening ear. Here, the patience learned from my father became a valuable asset as I taught important life lessons and helped to guide students by holding forums on the following topics: conflict resolution, empathy, positive peer interaction, self-assessment, the importance of non-verbal communication, self- and collective responsibility, bullying, respect for self and others, self-esteem issues, drug usage, time management, organizational and planning skills, confidentiality, relationship skills, teamwork, diversity, identity, life purpose, goal setting, and peer influences.

Whereas 70 percent of my students were considered at risk, the other 30 percent, mainly white, were academically successful. Nevertheless, they needed emotional nurturance. Through word of mouth, they heard I loved and cared for all students and I was approachable and treated everyone with dignity and respect regardless of class, gender, race, or ethnicity when assisting them with countless concerns. Although each day my interactions with students presented new challenges, I found ways to problem solve and to assist them whenever and however possible. If I did not have the expertise, I accessed outside resources and helped to make sure students received the best available services.

I derived much satisfaction in motivating students to achieve academically and in assisting them to develop positive coping skills within the classroom and other settings during regular school hours. One of the most important and exciting undertakings of my position was its flexibility because it allowed me to direct student clubs, coach teams, tutor students, conduct group discussions, and to build positive relationships with my students outside of the regular school day. The time spent outside of school instruction became a powerful experience of learning and self-esteem building. In particular, students who could not compete successfully with the schools' official sports teams were included in my after-school activities, regardless of their skill sets. Each day I labored in this position, I felt the Lord had blessed me and the many wonderful souls who needed what God put inside of me. I was fully engaged with my students and gave of myself like the Bible said: "Empty yourself and love others as I have loved the world." Each morning, I rose for work with a joyful exuberance. I was filled with compassion, ambition, and what I thought was some sense of autonomy and empowerment to support, nurture, and to love my students in my dream job.

Too soon, I learned this was not the case. In the early spring of 2008, my dream job turned nightmarish. I remember that day well when the first intimation [of trouble] occurred and I felt that I would need greater autonomy over my destiny. Signs of spring were in the air, and I was feeling exuberant and anew in my profession as student support specialist when events took an unexpected sinister turn. As I walked to my classroom with fifteen of my middle school students, eight males and seven females, from the Choices Program to assist them with their studies, I was suddenly stopped by Principal A. Appearing annoyed at seeing so many students surrounding me, she asked in an accusatory tone as though I had violated some code of conduct, "Where are you going with so many kids?" I replied, "I am having my sessions with the students who need help with their homework and other concerns." Seemingly filled with suspicion of an ulterior motive, her lips hardened and her icy eyes danced with malice as she instructed us to relocate to the auditorium without offering an explanation. Once there, a heavy oppression seemed to brood upon the air as she handed out pencils and sheets of paper and instructed the students to write letters about why they came to Mr. James. Although I was quite stunned, baffled, and confused by her behavior, out of respect for her position, I remained silent. I did not ask her, "What are you doing?" or "Why?" But I wondered, what was the meaning of her question? What was her intent? As the principal, should I expect her to know my job responsibilities as a student support specialist? Why was she acting as if I had done something inappropriate? Other teachers and staff of different gender identities, races, and ethnicities frequently walked the hallways with their students, and some were even suspected of inappropriate behavior toward their students. I wondered why she had not approached any of them. As the only African American male staff member, why was I being singled out by this African American principal? Why were my students being singled out? Was it because they were primarily poor and low-income minorities? I had observed that Principal A's attitude toward these students was dismissive and uncompassionate, especially with young Black males. In fact, she was ill at ease by the way these largely African American students spoke, behaved, and dressed. She labeled them unsmart and incapable. In numerous verbal and nonverbal gestures, she conveyed they did not belong at this middle-class school. In her eyes, my students were seen as a problem rather than as a promise for tapping and grooming, and they felt and expressed such sentiments.

Throughout the ordeal, I stayed calm while students completed their letters. With Principal A, every bit of her demeanor expressed an arrogant bitterness that I should genuflect before her. Before departing the auditorium to continue our instructional session, I requested a copy of the letters for my record. Lo and behold, the letters turned out to be life changing and overwhelming as well as a blessing in disguise. I learned students came to me not only for assistance with their lessons but also for emotional, psychological, and social support. Additionally, they wrote I encouraged and inspired them to see and achieve beyond their present circumstances. Although the responses were similar, here are three examples to illustrate my point. I did not edit the letters of these three unidentified middle school students for spelling, grammar, or punctuation because I want the reader to hear their authentic voices and to see and feel their pressing academic, psychological, and social concerns and needs that I confronted and worked to address each day.

*Letter #1*

The reason why I'm come to choices is because I cannot let my friends or won't to become leaders down. Another reason why is because I'm also trying to be a gentlemen. Mr. James also push me the hardest to try to good. But I can't help it. See I try to be good but my friends keep calling my name in classes. I try to annoy [avoid] but I just can't. So that one of the reason why I come to Choices. Mr. James always tell me to come Choices to be a role model. Because a lot of people look up to me.

It also help me to keeping getting good grades. Mr. James help us with our grades a lot. So that one more reason. The finally reason is to stay off the street and trouble. I also I really want to spread this program all over the world that why I come to choices. Mr. James, my father.

*Letter #2*

Choices helps me do my homework. It help me express my feels and helps me to calm down with my angry because I do have a angryment [anger management] problem and I really don't like talking to no more so I came into express my feels. I also came here so I want get in anymore trouble for the rest of the year. It teaches me what coming next in high school. It helps me not to think about the drama that goes on basely [basically] he said she said. Which its not worth so comeing [coming] here and talking about it help me think about how it not worth it.

    Mr. James talks about how not to take my angry out on other people and not getting kicked outer skool [school] because it. Me becomeing [becoming] a ninth grade year its not worth it doing all with hurt me and making me mad.

*Letter #3*

Choices help my [me] with doing my homework. Sometimes when I'm at home I don't feel like doing my homework. But in this class I have no choice but to do work. I also learn about not being a bully and gossip and other things that go on during school. He talks about different problems that we have and tries to help us.

    Choices is also like a tutoring class because if you don't know something then there is always someone who knows how. Another reason why choices is a good program because it helps you out if you need help. He also tries to correct you before you get into trouble. I come to choices also because I may need help doing something or I may have a problem. Choices gives you a choice from doing good and doing bad. Choices can also teach you about having a lesson on gossip. Because gossip can get a lot of people into trouble. Gossip can cause fights so he tries to stop it before it happens. Choices is a prevention class. He tries to prevent things before it happens because he don't want to see you get into trouble.

Although I was amazed at the students' responses, I also believed Principal A was as well. At that moment, I felt on top of the world, knowing she underestimated me. Yet I wondered why she had felt threatened by my presence as a Black male who enjoyed widespread support and influence among students. Interestingly, the principal had no further interaction with me regarding this incident. This occurrence, however, made it clear that Principal A's hostile attitude and behavior toward my students, who had come from underresourced backgrounds and who were clearly in greater need of nurturing to thrive successfully, contributed to the feeling that she thought helping them was, a waste of taxpayers' dollars. I vowed that day not to let her act of bad faith or other like-minded individuals who do not have the interests of students at heart to deter me. I will not change my stance. I will continue to move forward even in the face of resistance. The students' responses let me know that I was a good fit for their needs and concerns, and I must do whatever is necessary to create hope for thousands of youths, especially African Americans.[7] Although I was not a certified teacher, my role as a student support specialist served the function of being a role model and helped students to dream larger dreams.[8] What was in Principal A's mind can only be left to conjecture. As a role model for students, did she view my presence as a positive prototype or as a stereotypical threat? Judging from her verbal and behavioral reproach, my presence was troublesome, and in her eyes, she could only see a threatening six feet three inches, 275 pound, sexually threatening African American man. If that was her opinion, it was not my perspective. I was not there to be cute. I was there to serve my students. I was there to represent my father and mother and their collective values of education, service, accountability, hard work, fair play, respect, integrity and honesty, compassion, empathy, and most important, agape love.

Even though everyday racism continued throughout my time as a student support specialist, I ignored most of it. However, a few occasions really stood out. I am reminded of a frequent occurrence after I was reassigned to a high school that served primarily middle-class white students, although low-income students were enrolled. Each day after my students departed the school bus and entered the hallway, I was there to make them feel welcome. I felt very adamant about welcoming them with a warm, friendly smile since greeting and encouraging students was not only my forte, but it was also a strategy that I employed to promote school attendance and retention in an environment that was often hostile to them. Students reported being called dumb or called a racial or ethnic slur. Often, they overheard teachers talking to one another about them, so I wanted them to feel a sense of belonging and to let them know someone cared. Additionally, I wanted to serve as a role model for my students; therefore, I was always dressed in a neatly pressed suit and tie. I could hear echoes of my parents' voice that you must always look your best and be on your best behavior. Noting my influence with the students, what I encountered from my white colleagues were questions such as, "Why are you always dressed that way?" "What is your role in the school?" One white male instructor with whom I was not acquainted or, in fact, had not ever seen asked me, "Are you trying to be the principal?" I thought to myself, "What was his problem?" These countless everyday racist and gendered occurrences were commonplace. Some I challenged; at other times, I remained mute.

This next incident really leaps out at me. One day when I reported to the executive director of alternative education, she called me into her office to show me an email on her computer. "I need to show you something on my computer screen," she said. I approached her desk and proceeded to look at the information. She said, "This is from [Principal B of X School], one of the schools where you work." It read, "There are always students looking for Mr. James throughout the day all the time, and most of them are always girls." I wondered, "What was Principal B implying? Why was she unable to share this information face-to-face with me?" I had received only positive evaluations and feedback from my work with students. And certainly, no one had ever accused me of acting inappropriately, so what was the meaning of her email? At the end of the year, the executive director, who was rather positive and fair-minded toward my work with students, reassigned me to another school. My emotions ran the gamut because I knew students with whom I had bonded would be highly disappointed, especially since it would take considerable time to establish rapport with an adult whom they comfortably trusted. Unabashedly, I made it known that I loved and cared for my students as if they were my own, and I often communicated that care through social media. To love them was my way of encouraging students to succeed academically, to improve retention, and to encourage prosocial behavior. This was also my official job description, but agape love definitely did not have a place in the equation of this unsupportive environment for reaching and teaching poor and low-income children of color.

During the summer of 2018, my agape love for my students became a very high price to pay as I alluded to at the beginning of my reflections. One of my students' mother informed the principal's office that I posted on Instagram that I loved and cared for her daughter. As previously indicated, I was responding to her daughter's message stating she loved me and was thankful to me for assisting with her problem of alcoholism. As a result of supporting the young woman in her struggle with alcohol and for also saying that I loved and cared for her, I was summoned to the Human Resources Office of the Virginia Beach City Public Schools. When I entered the office, two human resources specialists, a white man and his white woman assistant, both had grave authoritarian looks on their faces. Then the woman's scarlet lips curled cruelly as her inquiring tone clearly expressed disapproval. After asking about the incident, the man joined her queries: "Why are you telling this particular young lady that you love her?" I replied, "Ma'am and sir, I tell most of my students that I love and care for them. They have called me 'Dad,' 'Second Dad,' 'the father that I never had,' and 'Uncle Eric.' I didn't ask them to call me that." Her air was distinctly critical as she began to scan my Instagram account. To barricade the road to truth, she retrieved only pictures of young women students posing with me; she did not show the ones with young men students or those with both young men and women. For the record, my account was not private, and I was not trying to hide anything. So what was their angle? As I sat before them in my Sunday best, I felt a curious inexplicable uneasiness. The untidiness of her appearance, especially her hair, was in contrast to mine. Her stony eyes now literally blazed with savage fire as she glared at me as if I were some sort of criminal or child molester. This incident took place during the height of the #MeToo movement. I said, "Ma'am, I have been with this school system for twelve years, and my evaluations are flawless and outstanding. I would not hurt any of my students because I do love and care for them." She replied, "This is inappropriate, and we have to protect our kids." "What did she mean by protecting our kids? From what or from whom?" I thought. As I sat there with my thoughts running freely, a powerful agitation and anger gripped me. I was their protector from the likeness of the principals, teachers, and counselors who cared so little for my students' hearts and souls that they metaphorically enabled their dreams to be deferred. They doused their dreams in hopelessness. In this strange scenario and twist of history, I also thought, "Who has been the likely protector of Black girls or the Black girl's mother? Who has been the likely predator?" The two of them continued to show pictures of me with girls and not with the boys from my Instagram account as if building evidence for a case. Further, they pulled documents and social media guidelines as though I committed a major violation. But my only crime was that I cared too much and that I had high expectations and respect for Black and brown children from low-income backgrounds who were looking for a positive male role model with whom to identify. A helpless anger simmered in me as I experienced this moment of social injustice. Again, like the other two principals, these human resources representatives appeared threatened by a tall, African American man. I felt singled out because of my physical being and my God-given gift of connecting with students for their betterment in this society.

The human resources representative gave me the option to resign or get a lawyer. But then, the Holy Spirit took possession of me. I said, "Peace be still." I kept my composure after my life flashed before my eyes. What will people say about me? What will the students say when I don't return? What will I tell my loved ones? I cried out, "God, I am your child!" I respectfully resigned, after saying to myself I will figure this all out. My spirit was so laden, and I did not know what to do next. I exited the door of the Virginia Beach Public Schools Administration Building, not knowing that God had other plans for me.

After leaving the school system, I was at a low point in my life, but I could clearly see having greater control over my destiny was one of God's plans for me. I also believed that my divine ordinance was to continue to address the needs of youth in diverse communities who have few resources to help them become successful. This life calling had already been laid on my heart by God to let their problems become my problems. So where do I go from here? That question became all-consuming and vexing to my soul for a few months until I had a heart-to-heart talk with my niece Candace Harris, a business owner and business consultant. She assisted with my vision and helped to turn an idea, Touch A Life Academy, into reality. To help youth to become successful in life, building character, and teaching life skills are basic requirements. To do so, it is important to instill confidence and to provide them with an education in values. The core values of Touch A Life Academy are derived from my parental teachings. They include the following: loving one another, treating all people with respect, employing the principles of Jesus Christ, helping others if you are in a position to do so, maximizing your potential, doing the best you can with what you have, being grateful, being humble, speaking life and not death, having compassion for people, treating others like you want to be treated, obtaining all the education you can, using your God-given talents to serve the world, creating a good name for yourself, and operating out of love.

I believe that when you operate out of love, God opens doors that no man can. And that makes me think of the ultimate sacrifice and love that my parents made for their children, which was to prepare us for a better quality of life. They performed countless deeds that increased our likelihood for success, in an above-average way, by fulfilling our hierarchy of needs from physiological to self-actualization. They poured so much love into us so we could have a strong sense of identity. We can stand for something and not fall for anything. When I think about my parents' winning formula for raising twelve children, it was not only the collective value system instilled in us, but they also recognized our individual differences. Like my parents who recognized our individual needs and differences, my business of educating has a distinct advantage over similar ones because it is tailored to meet both the individual and collective needs of youth. In focusing on the specific needs of students, Touch A Life Academy works to establish a personal rapport to meet youths where they are in life. Simply stated, I am providing time, compassion, and energy for students who lack nurturing through mentoring and coaching in after-school programs and in other ways where they can be reached. Furthermore, youths who participate in my organization have an opportunity to build a long-lasting healthy partnership with the academy. The primary focus is not profit but people. The academy exists to touch and change lives. At present, Touch A Life Academy has contracted with Newport News Behavioral Health in Newport News, Virginia, to provide activities for youth in a long-term mental health facility. My organization also has weekly mentoring sessions with students in Norfolk, Virginia.

It is my ultimate goal to operate Touch A Life Academy full time and to create employment opportunities for others. The academy plans to offer online services to support youth, to develop a speakers' bureau, and to mentor at schools, churches, and after-school programs. More important, I desire to operate my own facility to bring hope to youth across the nation and the world, but it must first start in my local communities. I have faith that it is going to happen. My father kept the faith when the doctor pronounced that I would not survive spinal meningitis as a three-month-old baby. Like my father, I kept the faith when I took care of him as a thirteen-year-old boy. Life did not get easier, but I got stronger and more resilient. When I think back to the day I exited the door of the Virginia Beach Public Schools Administration Building, I had faith, too, knowing God did not bring me this far to leave me. So I am paying it forward as I am moving forward. Since establishing Touch A Life Academy, I received my first service award from the Norfolk Alumnae Chapter of Delta Sigma Theta in 2021.

ROSCOE, SHIRLEY, AND ERIC have divergent stories leading to their entrepreneurial paths. Yet their narratives are convergent with reference to the influence of familial values transmitted by Pennie and Roscoe Sr. This is especially true in how they employ these values in coping with personal challenges and in incorporating them in their business model. As entrepreneurs, each has a strong penchant to serve others in a socially responsible way. Take stock of how Roscoe's youthful rebellion and more materialistic outlook subsided and evolved during incarceration. After his profound religious and spiritual conversion within the prison walls, his leadership abilities emerged. In adjusting to prison life, he viewed incarceration as an opportunity to better himself and to assist others. Criminologists refer to this process as gleaning. (See endnote 6 for further explanation.) Working through his youthful difficulties, he disengaged with some earlier values learned at the knee of his parents. In his internal discussion and role play with himself while isolated from his loving family, he reengaged with his familial values, in particular the communitarian and entrepreneurial spirit.

Next, in the conclusion, we look at how the Jameses' value system contributes to solidarity and how the family can maintain and culturally transmit solidarity from one generation to the next, along with the communitarian and entrepreneurial spirit.

# Conclusion

At the time I blurted out to Samuel James that I wanted to interview him during my visit to NASA on October 21, 2017, he was the sole focus of my inquiry. It was unimaginable that his multigenerational family members—mother, siblings, children, nieces, and nephews—would also be included in my investigation. To my delight, not only did the inclusion of family members have unintended consequences; its end results have been a meaningful and transformative journey for myself and for members of the family. Readers who take the James family's excursion find themselves looking through an interior lens of intergenerational collective narratives and riveting memories about solidarity and the communitarian and enterprising spirit. In the readers' angle of view is a frame of the James family. When they peer further inside the lens, they can see the homogeneity of their positive familial interactions. It is manifested through their enduring values of faith, family, respect, service, empowerment, strong work ethic, education, optimism, and noble character of accountability, ethics of care, kindness, love, loyalty, generosity, and strength. Having these values as interconnected cornerstones of their being have helped strengthen the familial patterns of solidarity embodied by the James clan, a seemingly fading cultural and social archetype. Perhaps such family togetherness will inspire others to reflect on their families, especially since a preponderance of dysfunctional families too often captures the awareness of social scientists and the media. We can begin this reflective positive path toward family functioning with two questions: First, what larger social inferences can be drawn from the Jameses' moving story of solidarity and its corollaries of communitarian and enterprising spirit? Second, is there an applicable theoretical framework for understanding how multigenerational families sustain cohesiveness over time?

Vern L. Bengtson and his colleagues appear to have an answer. After constructing a formal theory and testing it over several years, they provided a multidimensional paradigm for understanding intergenerational relations. It includes the following intergenerational solidarity taxonomy of six elements extracted from their research: associational solidarity, affectual solidarity, consensual solidarity, functional solidarity, normative solidarity, and structural solidarity.[1] The taxonomy of the six elements of intergenerational solidarity includes both nominal definitions and empirical indicators. For example, the construct of associational solidarity is defined as frequency and patterns of interaction during activities with family members. It is then measured through frequency of intergenerational interaction and the types of common activities. Affectual solidarity is defined as type and degree of positive sentiments among family members, measured through ratings of affection, warmth, and closeness. Consensual solidarity addresses the agreement on values, attitudes, and beliefs and is measured through intrafamilial consistency among individual indictors of values, attitudes, and beliefs. Next, functional solidarity is defined as the degree of helping and exchanging resources. This construct has an empirical indicator of intergenerational exchanges of assistance. Finally, normative solidarity refers to strength of commitment to family roles as measured through ratings of importance, while structural solidarity addresses opportunity structure with residential nearness, health, and number of family members.[2]

Bengtson and his collaborators' six constructs suitably encapsulate the lived experience of solidarity among three generations of the James family. Take, for example, the element of affectual solidarity expressed by the James siblings. When asked, "In thinking about your family prior to the series of interviews and/or reading about your family story, what descriptive words come to mind?" Of the eight siblings who responded to the follow-up questionnaire, each expressed positive sentiments to portray family relations. The warmth of words gushed forth like a blazing blue sky, pouring down torrents of light. The following are examples of words and phrases: anointed, love, God's children, unity, power, faith, perseverance, strength, prayerful, tenacious, committed, faithful, humorous, respect, giving, pleasant, amused, humble, kind, strong, talented, funny, popular, blessed, compassionate, friendly, caring, respectful, happy, sharing, grateful, highly favored, loving, generous, and spiritual.

Similarly, when asked, "In thinking about your family after the series of interviews and/or reading about your family story, what descriptive words come to mind?" Seemingly, a thousand evanescent memories of joyful days filled them as they depicted overwhelmingly positive thoughts and emotions in this way: amazing, consistent, aligned, shared philosophies, unity, togetherness, reawakening, humorous, heritage of faith, perseverance, humble, respectful, unified, understanding, long suffering, highly blessed, mesmerized, entranced, elated, overjoyed, resilient, faithful, God loving, life changing, grateful, anointed, highly favored, spiritual, and just simply thankful, the Lord knows, I am. Telling and reading the story brought the family closer. Eric added, "I feel even closer to [siblings] because we are able to share more personal testimonies together. We have always been very, very, very close. We are very tightly knitted. When we take our last breath, that will separate us."

Eric's vivid and arresting testimony supports that solidarity is the soul of the James family's narrative vignettes. As the siblings shared their stories with one another, their empathy and care ethics heightened. Perhaps this occurred because the act of telling a narrative story or vignette is an interactive process and can serve many functions. Bonding serves one of several purposes. In their study "A Retrospective Consideration of Recreational Family Storytelling among Parents and Their Adult Children," Kelly Gagalis-Hoffman, Ramon B. Zabriskie, and Patty A. Freeman noted, for example, how sharing stories generates openings for family bonding through several functions: being entertaining, handling problematic topics or situations, transmitting beliefs and values, providing listeners role models to emulate, allowing the opportunity to take new perspectives, and mindfully initiating intimacy between family members.[3] Although the James family's ties were heretofore strong, the group interviews bolstered their associational and affectional solidarity. Prior to the interview, they regularly emailed, telephoned, texted, and visited, especially for those who lived in close proximity. However, one specific pattern of interaction changed significantly—that is, a conference call of all siblings increased from special occasions to weekly. Here, siblings have entered fully into another life-stage cycle where they not only share and reflect on their growing-up years together, but they also discuss unresolved past concerns as well as their present experiences as adults. This greater sharing has further elevated and deepened the relational dimensions.

In addition to bonding, storytelling can also function as an emancipatory process in assisting individuals to make meaning of their lives or pivotal life events. Additionally, telling stories can be transformative for the storyteller and the listeners. It can also help to serve as a means of resisting situations or justifying choices, as a mode of emoting and healing, as well as a way of reinforcing moral lessons and connecting generations. It can provide narrative identity development and a sense of well-being. Finally, storytelling can be validating and affirming of experiences. This latter function appears to have well served the James siblings. Simultaneously, it has helped to buttress all six elements of intergenerational solidarity, particularly associational solidarity, consensual solidarity, and affectional solidarity. When asked how reading your family story has impacted your siblings, Shirley responded with a profound and eager hopefulness: "I believe my brothers and sisters have always wanted a platform to express their experiences where they wouldn't be judged or our family circumstances wouldn't summon any biased opinions. I feel that being given this opportunity to share our memories of growing up in such a large, tight-knit family with a strict religious upbringing and no financial wealth has given us an emotional outlet and a deeper sense of humility."

Not only is storytelling validating for her and her siblings, but on a more personal note, reading the family story for Shirley denoted a kind of ineffable crown of splendor during their growing-up years: "I feel vindicated in the sense that reading the documented evidence in black and white of our struggles, trials, tribulations, and triumphs while growing up was not in vain but had a purpose. It helped to shape the type of servant leaders we are today." Specifically, she offered this example of her vindication: "I recall that my parents raised us to be respectful of people while in public and to treat people like we want to be treated. We were raised to always carry ourselves with pride. When I was a very young girl, I recall that kids in school would make fun of us because there were so many children in the family. But I couldn't understand what they were laughing about or thought was funny because I felt loved, protected, cared for, and valued growing up in my family."

Seeing their inscribed story for Samuel has not only been affirmatory but also emancipatory. "I have even more respect for my siblings after hearing their life experiences and encounters. Everyone has exhaled. And there is a calmness about them. Our belief in Christ, along with our relationship, has strengthened even more. It has given me a calmness, and I feel complete because someone has heard our story." Likewise, after seeing their penned story, a fortuitous series of exultant thoughts crossed Mary's mind, tempered with a mild and humbling air on the reactions of her siblings and herself.

They were, and still are all fascinated. They are in awe and in disbelief of the story about "us." To all of us, it is like a fairytale—a remarkable dream—has come alive and it is still, seemingly, in existence. Because of the stronghold of love that we have for one another and the morals taught by our parents, this dream, which seems to be when I read the story of my family, will continue until eternity. I'm extremely confident of this through the faith that I have in God and in this family. I am also terribly amused by the story of my family. It has left me speechless, astounded, reserved, and in a daze. I know how blessed I am to have such an amazing and loving family. But when I see how the magnitude of some of those blessings measure up from the past and present on paper, it has made me almost feel a sense of guilt for not being even more thankful than I am presently. I just don't feel worthy of all the wonderful accolades because as children, we were only doing what we were being taught by our parents. To say the least, I'm beholden to my parents.

Adding a personal thought, Mary wrote:

I find myself thanking God even more for the strength, determination, and spirituality bestowed upon my parents. They provided us with consistent love and care, and these traits are manifested in their twelve children. They never fell short of these attributes. I'm even more attentive to my mom when I visit home. Usually when I'm there, I'm cleaning, cooking, and doing anything to enhance our homestead, because I know doing these things make her happy. But now I reserve more time to sit down with her just for conversation, and I eliminate anything that would cause a distraction. She's a woman of substantial empowerment. Her faith in God and her love of her family help to keep her energized, and they also help her to overcome her natural ailments.

For Karen and Darlene, sharing and reading their family story had an unintended effect. Both desire to intentionally initiate a profounder intimacy of individual identity, though Karen still believes that strengthening existing bonds through faith and love take primacy. "Our story encouraged us to stay connected to each other and to keep God in the middle of that connection. And love, love, love one another." Personally, she would like the bonds formed during childhood to be set anew in a fresher and deeper way: "I would love to have a one-on-one conversation with each of my siblings and my mother. I would love to get beneath the surface. What makes them happy? What brings them joy? What are their deepest fears?" In the same way, Darlene acknowledged that the family story "makes me want to know more about each other, and to search our family tree and understand other siblings' desires and passion." Like previous siblings, she also mentioned, "We talk more to each other."

This refrain of being more interactive and feeling even closer to one another was also vocalized by Wayne and Eric in their rejoinder after reading the family narrative. Eric wrote, "I have witnessed my siblings become more transparent and vulnerable. It is very difficult to share some life situations, but they are necessary, so that we can understand each other's walk in life and lift each other up when needed. We are a very grateful bunch, and we represent the true meaning of family love." Their family story also encouraged and facilitated Eric and Wayne to make changes in their lives and to pursue more eagerly their desired goals. Wayne said the experience provided clarity: "It has inspired me to pursue the best in life. I have decided to continue my education and pursue a doctorate in higher education. It has also inspired me to invest in my children's education and knowledge about Jesus Christ." Whereas Wayne's interest is in pursuing more formal education to develop programs and policies to eventually assist students from pre-K to high school, Eric's interest is in dispensing his acquired knowledge. He developed an organization, Touch A Life Academy, which is designed to improve, enrich, empower, and direct the life of a child. He stated:

> I can't say enough about the timing of these events that have occurred. With starting my own business and doing what I was called to do by God, this family story has just propelled me into my calling. I am so excited about being able to be used by God to minister to his people.
>
> I don't fear speaking to people because I feel like what I have to say, they need or want to hear. This has prepared me for what is ahead, and what is to come. This is the inspiration I needed after I stepped out on faith to begin my very own outreach company. After putting good content out into the world via social media about my outreach business, my dreams have become a reality. The right people and organizations are beginning to request me to speak, and I have begun to evolve.

Without his family's love and support, his evolution might not have materialized in this manner. Eric is plainly mindful of paying a courtly homage of respect when he verbalized, "After I declared myself a motivational speaker, my family has become my root for all of my speeches. I dedicate every future speaking engagement to my siblings, my mother, and the late Roscoe James Sr."

Since family is the height of magnanimity and love for the Jameses, perhaps Debbie sees it from the vantage point of author Adrienne Morris, who thinks "family is like music, some high notes, some low notes, but always a beautiful song." So the beautiful song of solidarity and the music of today, tomorrow, and unforgotten years sounded again in Debbie's soul as she summed up all six elements of intergenerational solidarity that have created the close-knit family and sustained members through "some high notes and low notes." Recapping the musical refrain, she expressed, "We have always been known as a close-knit family. Now, we are closer than we have ever been. We recognize each of us is a beautiful gift from God, and He's the one who created us and put us together to reflect His love toward everyone." Taking the larger sweeps in the march of the mind, Debbie reiterated such things as the eye of their familial history sees:

> I have made special efforts to love even more, and to spend quality time with one another while we all are still living. I feel our common bond of faith truly stands out, and we can be honest and open with ourselves more than ever. We have three different generational gaps, but now we share and accept our thoughts and ideas from each generation.
>
> We share music and enjoy our own style of entertainment, and we reach out in the many ways we possibly can. That is, we wear each other's clothes and we come together as a whole to care more for our mother. We are even letting her be herself, regardless of her age and old-fashioned ways. We are understanding what a fine job she did raising twelve children, and she is just the epitome of how a mother should raise her children. She always wanted the best for her children.

Pennie "always wanted the best for her children," and so did Roscoe Sr. He wanted to give his children "a good name." These two ardent avowals represent the kernel of their bestowed legacy—an affirmative value system and worldview that promote family solidarity and the communitarian and enterprising spirit. The affirmations also reinforce their strong identity, resilient spirit, and family mission. How they actualize their mission, for example, has been told and retold by the James siblings in their collective narrative vignettes. So how important is it to pass on such familial legacy? Arguably, in an increasingly rootless society, it is vital to preserve one's familial heritage for the next generation in order to know the value of belonging to an intergenerational story larger than ourselves. Knowing failures and successes of ancestors' narratives can also build resilience and offer a sense of well-being. Hence, it is advantageous to pass on family stories, especially since family relationships across generations are becoming increasingly important. Bengtson postulated, "For many Americans, multigenerational bonds are becoming more important than nuclear family ties for well-being and support over the course of their lives."[4] Moreover, he suggested that intergenerational relations will become more crucial in the twenty-first century for three reasons: "(a) the demographic changes of population aging, resulting in 'longer years of shared lives' between generations; (b) the increasing importance of grandparents and other kin in fulfilling family functions; and (c) the strength and resilience of intergenerational solidarity, over time."[5]

Whether one's familial structure is intergenerational, nuclear, single parent, or blended, the James siblings also think it is essential to tell the family story for different reasons. For Eric, a positive functioning family can serve as a role model. "This is extremely important because there are many families who need to see what a [healthy] family structure looks like. Families are created to love and support each other. The structure has been damaged greatly, and we have gotten away from traditions. If we don't model healthy families for our kids, we will be setting them up for failure. Family is where everything, and I mean everything, begins." So for Debbie, telling the family story begins with its significance as an indispensable support system where myriads of needs are met. "For the most part, you know your family and are more comfortable with them than anyone else. In times of sickness, you want your family to care for you. When times are hard, you want to be able to go to family for support. You have a deeper kind of joy being with family that makes you feel loved, secured, and protected. My father had a saying, 'A family that prays together, stays together.' I have no doubt that's what has kept us close together, despite whatever we faced."

Samuel sees its necessity as "an outlet or vent for anything that may be stressing them inside." Whereas he thinks the family story serves as a stress reducer, Shirley believes it contributes to a wider angle of vision and greater bonding. "I believe it's very important because we must understand the story from everyone's lens individually, since we have different experiences, perspectives, influences, and our own individual beliefs. Hearing the different versions of our family story can help us to better understand each other and to tighten the bond even more." Similarly, Darlene thinks telling and knowing the family story can "add more value and one can understand and appreciate [siblings'] decisions and their purpose in life." She further noted that it can also contribute to support and increased self-esteem, adding, "You give hope, liberation, and encouragement to each other or other families, so you or your siblings can feel secure, reassured, worthy, and loved." For Karen, "sharing stories brings authenticity. It's very important to have a sense of family to develop an understanding of who you are."

Wayne and Mary recognized the significance of transmitting the family's historical identity. "These stories must be told in order for children to understand their family history. I believe that understanding your family will give you a better direction in life," Wayne contended. Mary added, "I think it is important for families to tell their stories, so they can preserve the family history for future generations, and its members can have an idea of their family background. The life span of the person that holds the most history in the family is unpredictable. Therefore, they may not live to share it with the next generation. It doesn't always have to be published, but it is important to have a draft of the family history, and it should be preserved in a safe place. That would be so rewarding and priceless."

Mary's view of keeping the familial story alive is not only for the next generation, but it is also a cautionary call to action and a reminder of an old African proverb, "When an elder dies, it is as if an entire library has burned to the ground." Consequently, Mary is heeding her own warning and is thinking of "some practical ways of preserving family legacies through lots of photos for photo albums and video footages of special occasions, or through visits in general, and most definitely through a diary or journal of the family background to preserve for safe keeping." Samuel advocates transcribing "favorite memories, family retreats, and videos." Similarly, Wayne feels "the preservation of legacies can be done by recording major events in a family history and sharing them with each generation."

No doubt Darlene, Eric, Karen, and Shirley acknowledge leaving a digital footprint or written history is imperative, but they, too, believe living the legacy is more vital. It is perhaps the reason why Darlene quickly asserted, "Continue to carry on the legacy through our actions." Eric brought attention to this viewpoint when he stated families can preserve their affirmative legacy "by instilling and transmitting those most important values down through the generations. We have to plant seeds and put children first, because eventually the older ones will expire, and that richness needs to be given away. The Bible says, 'Empty ourselves and love one another the best way we can.'" For Karen, planting seeds for the next generation is done by keeping "the stories alive, and by communicating and passing them on to the next generation." Shirley opined one way "families can preserve their legacies is to have deliberate and consistent activities together." Remembering this example, she wrote, "My father planned family prayer with us almost every night. That regimen was engrained in me. To this day, I feel it is the glue that has kept us united and interactive, and it has connected our souls. I feel that is why we are so strong, connected, positive, and happy, and why we thrive on each other's spiritual strength, intellect, and focus."

Tim O'Brien, an American novelist, believes "the remembering makes it now. And sometimes remembering will lead to a story, which makes it forever. That's what stories are for joining the past to the future. Stories are for those late hours in the night when you can't remember how you got from where you were to where you are. Stories are for eternity, when memory is erased, when there is nothing to remember except the story."[6]

And so I end with this endearing story of Pennie's enduring love for her family. As her ailing health continued to decline in late November 2020, this nightly ritual ensued between Pennie and Debbie, her second oldest daughter. Debbie tucked her safely in bed, kissed her cheek, held her hand tightly, and gave comfort care as she bid her mother good night. Pennie always mustered a smile to softly respond, "Good night! And tell all my children I love them." Pennie died on December 29, 2020. An old folk belief is everything comes in threes, fortunes or fates. Fate landed again on the doorstep of the James family when Lubertha, the oldest sibling, died less than three weeks later on January 18, 2021, and two months later, Karen, the sixth sibling, died on March 23, 2021. "When there is nothing else to remember," let the Jameses' story of family love be a legacy and an eternal light for humanity.

Roscoe James Sr.
Courtesy of Samuel James.

Pennie James.
Courtesy of Samuel James.

Lubertha James.
Courtesy of Samuel James.

Debbie Simmons.
Courtesy of Samuel James.

Mary Wynn.
Courtesy of Samuel James.

Roscoe James Jr.
Courtesy of Samuel James.

Darlene James.
Courtesy of Samuel James.

Karen James.
Courtesy of Samuel James.

Shirley Dickerson.
Courtesy of Samuel James.

Samuel James.
Courtesy of Samuel James.

Wayne James.
Courtesy of Samuel James.

Beverly James.
Courtesy of Samuel James.

Terri James.
Courtesy of Samuel James.

Eric James.
Courtesy of Samuel James.

# Notes

## Prologue

1. Albert Mehrabian, *Silent Messages* (Belmont: Wadsworth, 1971), 43–44.
2. See Kristin Layous, S. Katherine Nelson, Jaime L. Kurtz, and Sonja Lyubomirsky, "What Triggers Prosocial Effort? A Positive Feedback Loop between Positive Activities, Kindness, and Well-Being," *Journal of Positive Psychology* 12, no. 4 (July 2017): 385–98, http://doi.org/10.1080/17439760.2016.1198924; Melanie Rudd, Jennifer Aaker, and Michael Norton, "Getting the Most Out of Giving: Concretely Framing a Prosocial Goal Maximizes Happiness," *Journal of Experimental Psychology* 54 (September 2014): 11–24, http://doi.org/10.1016/j.jesp.2014.04.002; Sue Kraus and Sharon Sears, "Measuring the Immeasurables: Development and Initial Validation of the Self-Other Four Immeasurables (SOFI) Scale Based on Buddhist Teachings on Loving Kindness, Compassion, Joy, and Equanimity," *Social Indicators Research* 92, no. 1 (May 2009): 169–81, https://doi.org/10.1007/s11205-008-9300-1; Andrea Malin, "Maximum Joy," *Prevention* 55, no. 9 (September 2003): 116–88; Lee Rowland and Oliver Scott Curry, "A Range of Kindness Activities Boost Happiness," *Journal of Social Psychology* 159, no. 3 (2019): 340–43; Keiko Otake, Satoshi Shimal, Junko Tanaka-Matsumi, Klanako Otsuji, and Barbara L. Fredrickson, "Happy People Become Happier through Kindness: A Counting Kindness Intervention," *Journal of Happiness Studies* 7, no. 3 (September 2006): 361–75; Janet Martin Soskice, *The Kindness of God: Metaphor, Gender, and Religious Language* (Oxford: Oxford University Press, 2007).
3. Michel Bourdeau, "Auguste Comte," *Stanford Encyclopedia of Philosophy* (Fall 2020), ed. Edward N. Zalta (plato.stanford.edu/archives/fall2020/entries/comte/).
4. William Du Bois and R. Dean Wright, "What Is Humanistic Sociology?" *American Sociologist* 33, no. 4 (Winter 2002): 12. See also Zakiya Luna and Whitney N. Laster Pirtle, eds., *Black Feminist Sociology: Perspectives and Praxis* (New York: Routledge, 2021); Marcus Hunter, ed., *The New Black Sociologists: Historical and Contemporary Perspectives* (New York: Routledge, 2018); Mario Luis Small and Jessica McCrory Calarco, *Qualitative Literacy: A Guide to Evaluating Ethnographic and Interview Research* (Berkeley: University of California Press, 2022); Margarita Mooney, *Faith Makes Us Live: Surviving and Thriving in the Haitian Diaspora* (Berkeley: University California Press, 2009).
5. John F. Glass, "Toward a Sociology of Being: The Humanistic Potential," *Sociology of Religion* 32, no. 4 (Winter 1971): 191–98, https://doi.org/10.2307/3710228.
6. Du Bois and Wright, "Humanistic Sociology," 6.
7. Du Bois and Wright, "Humanistic Sociology," 12.
8. Howard W. Odum, "Folk Sociology as a Subject Field for the Historical Study of Total Human Society and the Empirical Study of Group Behavior," *Social Forces* 31,

no. 3 (1953): 193–223, http://doi.org/10.2307/2574217; Mikkel Gerken, *On Folk Episte-mology: How We Think and Talk about Knowledge* (Oxford: Oxford University Press, 2017).

9. Steven Hitlin and Jane Piliavin, "Values: Reviving a Dormant Concept," *Annual Review of Sociology* 30 (2004): 359–93; Steven Hitlin and Stephen Vaisey, "The New Sociology of Morality," *Annual Review of Sociology* 39 (2013): 51–68; Talcott Parsons, "The Place of Ultimate Values in Sociological Theory," *International Journal of Ethics* 45, no. 3 (1935): 282–316; Milton Rokeach, *The Nature of Human Values* (New York: Free Press, 1973); Ronald Fischer and Ype H. Poortinga, "Are Cultural Values the Same as the Values of Individuals? An Examination of Similarities in Personal, Social and Cul-tural Values Structures," *International Journal of Cross-Cultural Management* 12, no. 2 (2012): 157–70; Geert Hofstede, *Culture's Consequences: Comparing Values, Behaviors, Institutions, and Organizations across Nations* (Thousand Oaks, CA: Sage, 2001); "The Concept of Values," in *International Encyclopedia of the Social Sciences*, ed. David L Sills (New York: Macmillan and Free Press, 1968), 16:283–87.

10. Du Bois and Wright, "Humanistic Sociology," 31–32.

11. Frederick Tse-shyang Chen, "The Confucian View of World Order," in *The Influence of Religion on the Development of International Law*, ed. Mark W. Janis (Leiden: Martinus Nijhoff, 1991).

## Chapter Two

1. Joseph F. Kett, "Reflections on the History of Adolescence in America," *History of Family* 8, no. 3 (2003): 355–73; G. Stanley Hall, *Adolescence: Its Psychology and Its Relations to Physiology, Anthropology, Sociology, Sex, Crime, Religion, and Education*, 2 vols. (New York: D. Appleton, 1904).

2. Pierre Bourdieu, "The Forms of Capital," in *Handbook of Theory and Research for the Sociology of Education*, ed. John G. Richardson (Westport, CT: Greenwood, 1986), 241–58; Scott Davies and Jessica Rizk, "The Three Generations of Cultural Capital Research: A Narrative Review," *Review of Educational Research* 88, no. 3 (June 2018): 331–65; James S. Coleman, "Social Capital in the Creation of Human Capital," *American Journal of Sociol-ogy* 94 (1988): S95–S120; John Field, *Social Capital*, 3rd ed. (London: Routledge, 2017). Cultural capital is not only class based, but it is also racialized. See Ashleigh Cart-wright, "A Theory of Racialized Cultural Capital," *Sociological Inquiry* 92, no. 2 (May 2022): 317–40; B. Brian Foster, *I Don't Like the Blues: Race, Place, and the Backbeat of Black Life* (Chapel Hill: University of North Carolina Press, 2020); Joseph C. Ewoodzie, *Getting Something to Eat in Jackson: Race, Class, and Food in the American South* (Princeton, NJ: Princeton University Press, 2021).

3. Christopher E. Beaudoin, "New Effects on Bonding and Bridging Social Capital: An Empirical Study Relevant to Ethnicity in the United States," *Communication Re-search* 38, no. 2 (April 2011): 155–78; Stephen A. Small, "Bridging Research Practice in the Family and Human Sciences," *Family Relations* 54 (April 2005): 320–34; Bingqing Wang, Laramie Taylor, and Qiusi Sun, "Families That Play Together Stay Together: Investigating Family Bonding through Video Games," *News Media and Society* 20, no. 11 (November 2018): 4074–94; Trevor H. Cairney, "Bridging Home and School

Literacy: In Search of Transformative Approaches to Curriculum," *Early Child Development and Care* 172, no. 2 (April 2002): 153–72; Robin L. Jarrett, Stephanie R. Jefferson, and Jenell N. Kelly, "Finding Community in Family: Neighborhood Effects and African American Kin Networks," *Journal of Comparative Family Studies* 41, no. 3 (2010): 299–328; Toby L. Parcel, Mikaela J. Dufur, and Rena Cornell Zito, "Capital at Home and at School: A Review and Synthesis," *Journal of Marriage and Family* 72, no. 4 (2010): 828–46; Toby L. Parcel and Mikaela J. Dufur, "Capital at Home and at School: Effects on Child Social Adjustment," *Journal of Marriage and Family* 63, no.1 (February 2001): 32–47. For a more in-depth analysis and discussion of the strengths of Black families and their enduring values, see Andrew Billingsley, *Climbing Jacob's Ladder: The Enduring Legacy of African-American Families* (New York: Simon & Schuster, 1992); Robert Hill, *The Strengths of Black Families* (New York: Emerson Hall, 1972); Joyce Ladner, *The Ties That Bind: Timeless Values for African American Families* (New York: Wiley, 1998); Harriet P. McAdoo, *Black Families* (Beverly Hills, CA: Sage, 1981). Although these works do not specifically discuss Black values as a form of social capital, it is implicit in the assumptions of the authors.

## Chapter Three

1. Julia Bryan, Raquel Farmer-Hinton, Anita Rawls, and Chenoa S. Woods, "Social Capital and College-Going Culture in High Schools: The Effects of College Expectations and College Talk on Students' Postsecondary Attendance," *Professional School Counseling* 21, no. 1 (2017–2018): 95–107; Julia Bryan, Cheryl Moore-Thomas, Norma L. Day-Vines, and Cheryl Holcomb-McCoy, "School Counselor as Social Capital: The Effects of High School Counseling on College Application Rates," *Journal of Counseling and Development* 89, no. 2 (Spring 2011): 190–99.

2. See chapter 2, "Education for Living and Uplifting," in Lois Benjamin, *Three Black Generations at the Crossroads: Community, Culture, and Consciousness*, 2nd ed. (Lanham, MD: Rowman & Littlefield, 2007).

3. Laura M. Padilla-Walker and Gustavo Carlo, "Personal Values as a Mediator between Parent and Peer Expectations and Adolescent Behaviors," *Journal of Family Psychology* 21, no. 3 (September 2007): 538–41; Eric Dearing, Holly Kreider, and Heather B. Weiss, "Increased Family Involvement in School Predicts Improved Child-Teacher Relationships and Feelings about School for Low-Income Children," *Marriage and Family Review* 43, no. 3 & 4 (2008): 226–54; Toby L. Parcel and Monica S. Bixby, "The Ties That Bind: Social Capital, Families, and Children's Well-Being," *Child Development Perspectives* 10, no. 2 (2016): 87–92; Jerome E. Morris, "Bonding Black Students, Families, and Community Socioculturally," *Educational Digest* 68, no. 5 (January 2003): 30–36; Wyletta Gamble-Lomax, *The Lived Experience of African American Women Mentors: What It Means to Guide as Community Pedagogues* (Lanham, MD: Lexington Books, 2016); Susan M. Sheridan and Lorey A. Wheeler, "Building Strong Family-School Partnerships: Transitioning from Basic Findings to Possible Practices," *Family Relations* 66, no. 4 (October 2017): 670–83.

4. Robert Putnam, *Bowling Alone: The Collapse and Revival of American Community* (New York: Simon & Schuster, 2000).

5. Jan-Walter De Neve and Ichiro Kawachi, "Spillovers between Siblings and from Offspring to Parents Are Understudied: A Review and Future Direction for Research," *Social Science and Medicine* 183, issue C (2017): 56–61; Lamont A. Flower, H. Richards Milner, and James L. Moore III, "Effects of Locus of Control on African American High School Seniors' Educational Aspirations: Implications for Preservice and Inservice High School Teachers and Counselors," *High School Journal* 87, no. 1 (October/November 2003): 39–50.

6. James S. Coleman, "Social Capital in the Creation of Human Capital," *American Journal of Sociology* 94 (1988): S95–S120.


Chapter Four

1. Bruce Feiler, "The Stories That Bind Us," *New York Times*, March 15, 2013, ST 1. Eva Gullov, Charlotte Palludan, and Ida Wentzel Winther, "Engaging Siblingships," *Childhood* 22, no. 4 (2015): 506–19.

2. Susan M. McHale, Kimberly Updegraff, and Shawn D. Whiteman, "Sibling Relationships and Influence in Childhood and Adolescence," *Journal of Marriage and Family* 74, no. 5 (October 2012): 913–30.

3. Nicole Campione-Barr, "The Changing Nature of Power, Control, and Influence in Sibling Relationships," *New Directions for Child and Adolescent Development*, no. 156 (Summer 2017): 7–14; Samantha A. Sang and Jackie A. Nelson, "The Effect of Siblings on Children's Social Skills and Perspective Taking," *Infant and Child Development* 26, no. 6 (2017): e2023.

4. Joe M. Chelladurai, David C. Dollahite, and Loren D. Marks, "'The Family That Prays Together . . .': Relational Processes Associated with Regular Family Prayer," *Journal of Family Psychology* 32, no. 7 (October 2018): 849–59.

5. McHale, Updegraff, and Whiteman, "Sibling Relationships and Influences in Childhood and Adolescence"; Shawn D. Whiteman, Julia M. Becerra Bernard, and Susan M. McHale, "The Nature and Correlates of Sibling Influence in Two-Parent African American Families," *Journal of Marriage and Family* 72, no. 2 (April 2010): 267–81.

6. McHale, Updegraff, and Whiteman, "Sibling Relationships and Influences in Childhood and Adolescence."

7. Frederick Buechner, *A Room Called Remember: Uncollected Pieces* (New York: HarperCollins, 1992), 6.

8. Yung-Chi Chen and Marian C. Fish, "Parental Involvement of Mothers with Chronic Illness and Children's Academic Achievement," *Journal of Family Issues* 34, no. 5 (May 2013): 583–606; Yung-Chi Chen, "Exploration of the Short-Term and Long-Term Effects of Parental Illness on Children's Educational and Behavioral Functioning Using a Large Taiwanese Sample," *Western Journal of Nursing Research* 36, no. 5 (May 2014): 664–84; Angeliki Bogosian, Rona Moss-Morris, and Julie Hadwin, "Psychosocial Adjustment in Children and Adolescents with a Parent with Multiple Sclerosis: A Systematic Review," *Clinical Rehabilitation* 24, no. 9 (September 2010): 789–801; Angeliki Bogosian, Julie Hadwin, Matthew Hankins, and Rona Moss-Morris, "Parents' Expressed Emotion and Mood, Rather Than the Physical Disability Are

Associated with Adolescent Adjustment: A Longitudinal Study of Families with a Parent with Multiple Sclerosis," *Clinical Rehabilitation* 30, no. 3 (March 2016): 303–11; Rose Marie Horner, "Interventions for Children Coping with Multiple Sclerosis: A Systematic Review," *Journal of the American Association of Nurse Practitioners* 25, no. 6 (June 2013): 309–13, https://doi.org/10.1111/j.1745-7599.2012.00795.x.

9. Katarzyna Kamilla Walecka-Matyja, "Relationship with Siblings as a Predictor of Empathy and Humor Styles in Early Adulthood," *Archives of Psychiatry and Psychotherapy* 19, no. 3 (2017): 48, 43–51.

10. Alejandro Portes, "Social Capital: Its Origins and Application to Modern Sociology," *Annual Review of Sociology* 24, no. 1 (August 1998): 1–24.

11. Young-Il Kim and Bradford W. Wilcox, "Bonding Alone: Familism, Religion, and Secular Civic Participation," *Social Science Research* 42, no. 1 (January 2013): 31–45; Jeremy Rhodes, "The Ties That Divide: Bonding Social Capital, Religious Friendship Networks, and Political Tolerance among Evangelicals," *Sociological Inquiry* 82, no. 2 (May 2012): 163–86; Kevin D. Dougherty, Fred J. De Jong, Rebecca L. Garofano, Jessika I. Jamir, Natalie J. Park, and Rebecca J. Timmermans, "Bonding and Bridging Activities of U.S. Pentecostals," *Sociological Spectrum* 31, no. 3 (May/June 2011): 316–41; W. Matthew Henderson, Brittany Fitz, and F. Carson Mencken, "Judgmental God Image, Social Embeddedness, and Social Trust among the Highly Religious in the United States," *Journal of Contemporary Religion* 32, no. 1 (January 2017): 1–14.

Chapter Five

1. Benjamin G. Gibbs, Lance D. Erickson, Mikaela Dufur, and Aaron Miles, "Extracurricular Associations and College Enrollment," *Social Science Research* 50 (March 2015): 367–81; Andrew Guest and Barbara Schneider, "Adolescents' Extracurricular Participation in Context: The Mediating Effects of School, Community, and Identity," *Sociology of Education* 76, no. 2 (April 2003): 89–102; Ralph B. McNeal Jr., "Participation in High School Extracurricular Activities: Investigating School Effects," *Social Science Quarterly* 80, no. 2 (June 1999): 291–309; Tony White, Lionel D. Scott Jr., and Michelle R. Munson, "Extracurricular Activity Participation and Educational Outcomes among Older Youth Transitioning from Foster Care," *Children and Youth Services Review* 85 (January 2018): 1–8; Jennifer Schmidt, Lee Shumow, and Hayal Kackar-Cam, "Adolescents' Participation in Service Activities and Its Impact on Academic, Behavioral, and Civic Outcomes," *Journal of Youth and Adolescence* 36, no. 2 (2007): 127–40; Jan N. Hughes, Qian Cao, and Oi-man Kwok, "Indirect Effects of Extracurricular Participation on Academic Adjustment via Perceived Friends' Prosocial Norms," *Journal of Youth and Adolescence* 45, no. 11 (November 2016): 2260–77; Andrew Martinez, Crystal Coker, Susan D. McMahon, Jonathan Cohen, and Amrit Thapa, "Involvement in Extracurricular Activities: Identifying Differences in Perceptions of School Climate," *Educational and Developmental Psychologist* 33, no. 1 (July 2016): 70–84, https://doi.org/10.1017/edp.2016.7; H. David Hunt, "The Effect of Extracurricular Activities in the Educational Process: Influence on Academic Outcomes?" *Sociological Spectrum* 25, no. 4 (July 2005): 417–45; Ann Meier, Benjamin Swartz Hartmann, and Ryan Larson, "A Quarter Century of Participation in School-Based Extracurricular Activities: Inequality

by Race, Class, Gender and Age?" *Journal of Youth and Adolescence* 47, no. 6 (June 2018): 1299–316; Herbert W. Marsh and Sabina Kleitman, "Extracurricular School Activities: The Good, the Bad, and the Nonlinear," *Harvard Educational Review* 72, no. 4 (Winter 2002): 464–515; Jennifer A. Fredricks and Jacquelynne S. Eccles, "Breadth of Extracurricular Participation and Adolescent Adjustment among African-American and European-American Youth," *Journal of Research on Adolescence* 20, no. 2 (2010): 307–33; Jennifer A. Fredricks and Jacquelynne S. Eccles, "Is Extracurricular Participation Associated with Beneficial Outcomes? Concurrent and Longitudinal Relations," *Developmental Psychology* 42, no. 4 (July 2006): 698–713.

2. George Farkas, "Cognitive Skills and Noncognitive Traits and Behaviors in Stratification Processes," *Annual Review of Sociology* 29, no. 1 (2003): 541–62; Matthew Hall and George Farkas, "Adolescent Cognitive Skills, Attitudinal/Behavioral Traits and Career Wages," *Social Forces* 89, no. 4 (June 2011): 1261–85.

3. Jessica F. Harding, Pamela A. Morris, and Diane Hughes, "The Relationship between Maternal Education and Children's Academic Outcomes: A Theoretical Framework," *Journal of Marriage and Family* 77, no. 1 (February 2015): 60–76.

4. James Moore, "A Challenge for Social Studies Educators: Increasing Civility in Schools and Society by Modeling Civic Virtues," *Social Studies* 103, no. 4 (July/August 2012): 140–48; Michael P. Leiter, Sheri L. Price, and Heather K. Spence Laschinger, "Generational Differences in Distress, Attitudes, and Incivility among Nurses," *Journal of Nursing Management* 18, no. 8 (November 2010): 970–80.

5. Keith Zabel, Benjamin Biermeier-Hanson, Boris Baltes, Becky J. Early, and Agnieszka Shepard, "Generational Differences in Work Ethic: Fact or Fiction," *Journal of Business and Psychology* 32, no. 3 (June 2017): 301–15; Jean M. Twenge, "A Review of the Empirical Evidence on Generational Differences in Work Attitudes," *Journal of Business and Psychology* 25, no. 2 (June 2010): 201–10; Brenda Kowske, Rena Rasch, and Jack Wiley, "Millennials' (Lack of) Attitude Problem: An Empirical Examination of Generational Effects on Work Attitudes," *Journal of Business and Psychology* 25, no. 2 (June 2010): 265–79; John Meriac, David Woehr, and Christina Banister, "Generational Differences in Work Ethic: An Examination of Measurement Equivalence across Three Cohorts," *Journal of Business and Psychology* 25, no. 2 (June 2010): 315–24.

6. Max Weber, *The Protestant Ethic and the Spirit of Capitalism* (New York: Scribner, 1958).

7. Kevin Cokley, Meera Komarraju, Rachael Pickett, Frances Shen, Nima Patel, Vinetha Belur, and Rocio Rosales, "Ethnic Differences in Endorsement of Protestant Work Ethic: The Role of Ethnic Identity and Perceptions of Social Class," *Journal of Social Psychology* 147, no. 1 (2007): 76, 75–89.

8. Cokley et al., "Ethnic Differences," 76.

9. Cokley et al., "Ethnic Differences," 76.

10. See William E. Cross, "Models of Psychological Nigrescence: A Literature Review," in *Black Psychology*, ed. Reginald L. Jones (New York: Harper and Row, 1980); Beverly J. Vandiver, Peony E. Fhagen-Smith, Kevin O. Cokley, William E. Cross Jr., and Frank C. Worrell, "Cross's Nigrescence Model: From Theory to Scale," *Journal of Multicultural Counseling and Development* 29, no. 3 (July 2001): 174–200.

## Chapter Six

1. Casey E. Copen and Merril Silverstein, "The Transmission of Religious Beliefs across Generations: Do Grandparents Matter?" *Journal of Comparative Family Studies* 39, no. 1 (Winter 2008): 59–71.

2. Vern L. Bengtson, Casey E. Copen, Norella M. Putney, and Meril Silverstein, "A Longitudinal Study of the Intergenerational Transmission of Religion," *International Sociology* 24, no. 3 (May 2009): 325–45.

3. Sarah K. Spilman, Tricia K. Neppl, M. Brent Donnellan, Thomas J. Schofield, and Rand D. Conger, "Incorporating Religiosity into a Developmental Model of Positive Family Functioning across Generations," *Developmental Psychology* 49, no. 4 (April 2013): 762–74; David C. Dollahite, Loren D. Marks, Kate P. Babcock, Betsy H. Barrow, and Andrew H. Rose, "Beyond Religious Rigidities: Religious Firmness and Religious Flexibility as Complementary Loyalties in Faith Transmission," *Religions* 10, no. 2 (2019): 111, https://doi.org/10.3390/rel10020111.

4. Douglas L. Flor and Nancy Flanagan Knapp, "Transmission and Transaction: Predicting Adolescents' Internalization of Parental Religious Values," *Journal of Family Psychology* 15, no. 4 (2001): 627–45; Jungmeen Kim-Spoon, Gregory S. Longo, and Michael E. McCullough, "Parent-Adolescent Relationship Quality as a Moderator for the Influences of Parents' Religiousness on Adolescents' Religiousness and Adjustment," *Journal of Youth and Adolescence* 41, no. 12 (2012): 1576–87.

5. Michael Bond, "Why Money Can't Buy You Love: The Unexpected Price of Wealth," *New Scientist* 214, no. 2861 (April 21, 2012): 52–55.

6. Rochelle Parks-Yancy, "The Effects of Social Group Membership and Social Capital Resources on Careers," *Journal of Black Studies* 36, no. 4 (March 2006): 515–45.

7. Gail Lumet Buckley, *The Hornes: An American Family* (New York: Applause, 2002), 4.

8. Pearl S. Buck, *To My Daughters with Love* (New York: John Day, 1967), 88.

9. Alex Haley, *The Man Who Traced America's Roots: His Life, His Works* (New York: Reader's Digest, 2007), 159.

## Chapter Seven

1. In Table 2.1 of chapter 2, the nine core values represent solidarity. Faith, family, and education are considered mediating variables for the enterprising spirit and the communitarian spirit. The former includes the conceptual dimensions of optimism, empowerment, and the work ethic. The latter includes the conceptual dimensions of noble character, respect, and service. The descriptors/indicators are also identified in Table 2.1. I posit that having an enterprising spirit is more likely to lead to entrepreneurship and innovation, producing entrepreneurs who contribute to individual social mobility. In contrast, having a communitarian spirit is more likely to lead to a service orientation and an ethic of care, producing servant leaders who contribute to group social mobility. When both values are present, the likely outcome is socially responsible entrepreneurs who contribute to individual and group social mobility.

2. Pierre Bourdieu, "On the Family as a Realized Category," *Theory, Culture and Society* 13, no. 3 (1996): 19–26.

3. Bourdieu, "On the Family," 24; David Throsby, "Determining the Value of Cultural Goods: How Much (or How Little) Does Contingent Valuation Tell Us?" *Journal of Cultural Economics* 27, no. 3-4 (2003): 275–85; Melvin L. Kohn, Kazimierz M. Slomczynski, and Carrie Schoenbach, "Social Stratification and the Transmission of Values in the Family: A Cross-National Assessment," *Sociological Forum* 1, no. 1 (1986): 73–102.

4. One deeply ingrained assumption, largely supported by research findings, is that entrepreneurs have greater economic wealth than wage earners, although some more recent findings present a mixed picture. This is especially the case with small businesses. Thomas Astebro and Jing Chen, "The Entrepreneurial Earnings Puzzle: Mismeasurement or Real?" *Journal of Business Venturing* 29 (2014): 88–105.

5. Robert Smith, "Mentoring and Perpetuating the Entrepreneurial Spirit within Family Business by Telling Contingent Stories," *New England Journal of Entrepreneurship* 12, no. 2 (2009): 27.

6. Todd R. Clear, Michael D. Reisiq, and George F. Cole, *American Corrections*, 12th ed. (Boston: Cengage Learning, 2018), 284–85. John Irwin identified four major types of adjustments most males use to adapt to prison life: (1) Doing Time—Men "doing time" view their prison term as a brief, inevitable break in their criminal careers, a cost of doing business. (2) Jailing—The men are interested in cutting themselves off from the outside world and continuing their pattern of behavior developed in the outside world and are merely there doing time. (3) Gleaning—The men view prison as an opportunity to better themselves. (4) Disorganized Criminal—This describes people who cannot develop any of the other three role orientations. Roscoe's adjustment to incarceration can best be described as gleaning.

7. Chandra Thomas Whitfield, "Only Two Percent of Teachers Are Black Men, yet Research Confirms They Matter," *Undefeated* (January 29, 2019): 1–10, https://theundefeated.com/features/only-two-percent-of-teachers-are-black-men-yet-research-confirms-they-matter/. The literature indicates that students do better when they have role models with whom they can identify. Whitfield noted in the United States, the public schools comprise approximately 80 percent of white teachers, and about 77 percent of them are white female. Twenty percent are people of color. Black men comprise only 2 percent of all teachers in the public schools in the United States. Although other racial and ethnic groups can benefit from their presence, too often, these few serve primarily underresourced students, and they also are more likely to act as disciplinarians.

8. Jill Rosen, "Black Students Who Have at Least One Black Teacher Are More Likely to Graduate," *Johns Hopkins Magazine*, April 5, 2017, https://releases.jhu.edu/2017/04/05/with-just-one-black-teacher-black-students-more-likely-to-graduate/. A 2017 study coauthored by a Johns Hopkins University economist showed underresourced African American students who had at least one Black teacher were considerably more likely to graduate from high school and contemplate attending college.

## Conclusion

1. Vern L. Bengtson and Robert E. L. Roberts, "Intergenerational Solidarity in Aging Families: An Example of Formal Theory Construction, "*Journal of Marriage and*

*Family* 53, no. 4 (November 1991): 856–70; Vern L. Bengtson and Sandi S. Schrader, "Parent-Child Relations," *Research Instruments in Social Gerontology* 2 (1982): 115–86.

2. Bengston and Roberts, "Intergenerational Solidarity in Aging Families," 857. These six features of the intergenerational solidarity model have been empirically tested between generations, using a longitudinal study consisting of a cross section of 2,044 participants from three-generational families and at various intervals.

3. Kelly Gagalis-Hoffman, Ramon B. Zabriskie, and Patti A. Freeman, "A Retrospective Consideration of Recreational Family Storytelling among Parents and Their Adult Children," *Marriage and Family Review* 52, no. 4 (June 2016): 392–412.

4. Vern L. Bengtson, "Beyond the Nuclear Family: The Increasing Importance of Multigenerational Bonds," *Journal of Marriage and Family* 63, no. 1 (February 2001): 5, 1–16, http://doi.org/10.1111/j.1741-3737.2001.00001.x. See also Cheryl Waites, "Building on Strengths: Intergenerational Practice with African American Families," *Social Work* 54, no. 3 (2009): 278–87, http://doi.org/10.1093/sw/54.3.278.

5. Bengtson, "Beyond the Nuclear Family," 1.

6. Tim O'Brien, *The Things They Carried: A Work of Fiction* (Boston: Houghton Mifflin, 1990), 38.

# Index

Note: Page numbers in italics refer to figures.

James, Lubertha, *152*; care ethics of, 79–80, 90; death of, 149; education of, 63; family care by, 21, 44–45, 46, 50–51; illness of, 80–81; on Leon, 59–60; on racism, 84–85, 86; religious faith of, 8–9; on Roscoe Sr.'s faith, 41–42; on Roscoe Sr.'s generosity, 54

James, Machell, 116

James, Mary. *See* Wynn, Mary

James, Malissa, 5, 128

James, Pennie, *151*; bullying episode with, 60–61; care ethics of, 79–80; death of, 149; description of, 5; early life and family of, 20–21; family core values of, 22–24; family tree of, 26; parenting style and priorities of, 29, 31–32, 40–41, 70, 72–73, 146; pushback against the church by, 62–67; Samuel's description of, 15; strength of, 69–75; work ethic of, 75–76; work outside of the home of, 21–22

James, Roscoe, Jr., *153*; care ethics of, 81, 109, 117–18; on racism, 89–90; religious faith and work of, 55–56, 113–15, 138–39; on siblings' influence, 51–52; work of, 2, 109–10, 115–17; youthful rebellion of, 24, 110–13

James, Roscoe, Sr., *151*; care ethics of, 80–81; Darlene on, 53–54; death of, 24; early life and family of, 19–22; expressions of faith by, 48–49; expressions of joy by, 42–43; family core values of, 22–24; family tree of, 26; generosity of, 54; on giving his children a "good name," 20, 25, 39, 84, 91, 105, 146; home built by, 4; illness of, 57–58, 66, 110; Samuel's description of, 15, 20, 24–25, 35; work ethic of, 77, 78; work of, 20, 22, 30

James, Samuel, 1, *155*; description of, 15–16; description of Roscoe by, 15, 20, 24–25, 35; education of, 30–33; on family core values, 27–30; football and, 62–63; patents of, 14–15, 34–35, 37; racist slur against, 86–87; on sharing

family story, 143, 147, 148; Wayne's description of, 38–39; work at NASA, 14–15, 17, 33–37

James, Senya, 1, 38, 98–100

James, Shirley. *See* Dickerson, Shirley

James, Terri, 2, *157*; description of, 5; on discipline, 74; on experience of family love, 56; on gender restrictions, 66, 83; naming of, 45; on Pennie's strength, 69–70; racist epithet against, 87; on Roscoe's joy, 42

James, Valerie, 1, 38

James, Wayne, *156*; description of Samuel by, 38–39; on family values, 53; musical and educational pursuits of, 68–69, 71–72; on Pennie's work ethic, 75–76; on religious restrictions, 62, 65; retirement and impact as a teacher, 1–4; on Roscoe's joy, 42; on sharing family story, 145, 147; on student expectations, 73–74; on work ethic, 77, 78–79

journey of the soul, 9

joy, 42, 48–49, 75, 95–96. *See also* laughter

joyful giving, 59, 61

Keltner, Dacher, 100

Kennedy, John F., 14

kindness, 5, 12, 49, 98. *See also* care ethics

King, Martin Luther, Jr., 6

laughter, 45, 48, 49, 95. *See also* joy

L'Engle, Madeleine, 91

Little Rock Nine, 73

Lombardi, Vince, 75

marching band, 66–67

marriage, 21

Marx, Karl, 9

Mehrabian, Albert, 2

Mercury-Redstone rocket, 14

merit-based system, 7

Meyer, Danny, 5

Mills, C. Wright, 9, 10, 11

Mitchell, Jasmine, 126

Mitchell, Paige, 91, 92–94, 95, 96, 102, 126

money management, 76–77. *See also* financial independence
Morris, Adrienne, 145
musical talents, 4–5, 41, 66–67, 68, 111, 117
Myavana (brand), 101, 126

NASA Langley Research Center, 14, 33–37
nasal suction and irrigation prototype, 37–38
*New England Journal of Entrepreneurship* (publication), 108
*New Scientist* (publication), 100
Nigrescence model, 88
normative solidarity, 140, 141. *See also* solidarity
North Carolina Potato Festival, 4
Nouwen, Henri, 2

O'Brien, Tim, 148–49
Odum, Howard, 10–11

Parks-Yancey, Rochelle, 101
patents, 14–15, 34–35, 37
Picoult, Jodi, 91
*ping*, 13
police encounter, 87–88
Portes, Alejandro, 61
positivism, 9, 10
prayer, 46, 48, 94
pressure-assisted linear seal patent, 15
prison life, 166n6
privilege, 83, 93
Protestant work ethic, 78–79. *See also* work ethic

racial identity and racism, 83–90, 134–35, 160n2. *See also* class identity; cultural capital; ethnic identity
razor bumps and T-Stone patent, 37
recipes, 24
religious faith: biblical stories, 99; of Eric, 137–38; family prayer, 46, 48, 94, 147; family studies on, 91–92; of James family, 41–44; of Karen, 50; of Lubertha, 8–9; restrictive aspects of,

62–65; of Roscoe Jr., 55, 113–15, 138–39; of Roscoe Sr., 41–42, 48–49; of Samuel, 28–29; of Shirley, 122–26; on treating everyone equally, 82–90. *See also* Sunday rituals
research approach, 1–2, 4, 7–9, 17–18
resilience, 21, 43, 47, 48, 49, 59, 94, 104, 138, 146
respect, 6, 13, 53, 63, 82. *See also* treating everyone equally
"A Retrospective Consideration of Recreational Family Storytelling among Parents and Their Adult Children" (study), 142
*A Room Called Remember* (Buechner), 55
Rumi, 38

Sanctuary Global, 119
scientific positivism, 9, 10
segregation, 84–85
self-care, 101
self-discipline, 29–30. *See also* work ethic
self-discovery, 119–27
Self-Discovery with Shirley (business), 119, 125, 126
self-sufficiency, 77–78, 79. *See also* financial independence
self-worth, 103, 122, 126
service orientation, 109. *See also* civic participation; communitarian spirit
Sessoms, Leon, 59–60
sexuality, 82–83
Shakespeare, William, 43
Shepard, Alan, 14
Simmons, Debbie, 2, 67, 82, 145–46, 147, 152
Small, Albion, 9
Smith, Robert, 108
social capital, 25–26, 31–32, 38, 101, 106
sociological gaze, 7–8, 9–10. *See also* humanistic sociology
sociology of being, 9
solidarity, 24, 106–9, 140–42, 165n1 (ch. 7), 167n2. *See also* family bond
Sorokin, Pitirim A., 9